PURCELL

DIDO AND AENEAS

An Opera

An Authoritative Score

Historical Background · A Critical Edition of the Libretto

Criticism and Analysis · Production and Interpretation

NORTON CRITICAL SCORES

BACH **CANTATA NO. 4**
edited by Gerhard Herz

BACH **CANTATA NO. 140**
edited by Gerhard Herz

BEETHOVEN **SYMPHONY NO. 5 IN C MINOR**
edited by Elliot Forbes

BERLIOZ **FANTASTIC SYMPHONY**
edited by Edward T. Cone

CHOPIN **PRELUDES, OPUS 28**
edited by Thomas Higgins

DEBUSSY **PRELUDE TO "THE AFTERNOON OF A FAUN"**
edited by William W. Austin

HAYDN **SYMPHONY NO. 103 IN E-FLAT MAJOR ("DRUM ROLL")**
edited by Karl Geiringer

MOZART **PIANO CONCERTO IN C MAJOR, K. 503**
edited by Joseph Kerman

MOZART **SYMPHONY IN G MINOR, K. 550**
edited by Nathan Broder

PURCELL **DIDO AND AENEAS**
edited by Curtis Price

SCHUBERT **SYMPHONY IN B MINOR ("UNFINISHED")**
edited by Martin Chusid

SCHUMANN **DICHTERLIEBE**
edited by Arthur Komar

STRAVINSKY **PETRUSHKA**
edited by Charles Hamm

WAGNER **PRELUDE AND TRANSFIGURATION**
from *TRISTAN AND ISOLDE*
edited by Robert Bailey

Henry Purcell

DIDO AND AENEAS

An Opera

An Authoritative Score
Historical Background · A Critical Edition of the Libretto
Criticism and Analysis · Production and Interpretation

Edited by

CURTIS PRICE

KING'S COLLEGE LONDON

W · W · NORTON & COMPANY

New York · London

Composition by JGH Composition, Inc. Manufacturing by The Murray Printing Company.

FIRST EDITION

Library of Congress Cataloging in Publication Data
Purcell, Henry, 1659–1695.
[Dido and Aeneas]
(Norton critical scores)
Libretto by Nahum Tate.
1. Operas—Scores.   I. Price, Curtis Alexander, 1945–
II. Tate, Nahum, 1652–1715. lbt.   III. Title.   IV. Series.
M1500.P98D4   1986   86-750870

ISBN 0-393-02407-5

ISBN 0-393-95528-1 PBK.

W. W. Norton & Company, Inc., 500 Fifth Avenue, New York, N.Y. 10110
W. W. Norton & Company Ltd., 37 Great Russell Street, London WC1B 3NU
1 2 3 4 5 6 7 8 9 0

CONTENTS

Introduction   vii

Historical Background
    Curtis Price • *Dido and Aeneas* in Context   3
    A. Margaret Laurie • Allegory, Sources, and Early
                      Performance History   42

The Libretto: A Critical Edition   63
    Gildon's Conclusion of the Prologue (1700)   77
    Gildon's Insertion for the Grove Scene (1700)   78

The Score   83
    Michael Tilmouth • A Newly-Composed Finale for the
                      Grove Scene   183

Criticism and Analysis
    George Bernard Shaw • [A Trip to Bow]   191
    Andrew Porter • [British Worthy]   193
    Jack Westrup • [A Flawed Masterpiece]   195
    Wilfrid Mellers • The Tragic Heroine and the Un-Hero   204
    Edward J. Dent • [Recitative, Dance and Rhythm]   214
    Robert E. Moore • [*Dido and Aeneas* and Later Opera]   220
    Joseph Kerman • [A Glimmer from the Dark Ages]   224
    John Buttrey • [A Cautionary Tale]   228

The Missing Music Controversy: Another Point of View
Geoffrey Bush • [A Debate with Benjamin Britten]   239
Ellen T. Harris • [The Design of the Tenbury Manuscript]   243

Production and Interpretation
Roger Savage • Producing *Dido and Aeneas*   255

INTRODUCTION

Purcell's *Dido and Aeneas* is one of the greatest operas composed between Monteverdi's lifetime and Mozart's. Its potential to move modern audiences through tragic irony is almost unrivalled, even when acted by adolescents, as it was at the premiere in 1689. Yet it is in almost every way anomalous: a *tragic, English* opera created at a time when operas were hardly ever tragic and when England had no real opera. Partly for this reason, Purcell's masterpiece lay forgotten and unperformed for nearly one hundred years, was debased and disfigured in the nineteenth century, and has been alternately praised and belittled — often for the wrong reasons — since Edward Gordon Craig's landmark revival in 1900.

One of the reasons *Dido* has been so badly misunderstood is because it is usually deemed, incorrectly, to be the culmination of Purcell's stage career rather than a modest prolegomenon. His association with the professional theatre began, if one disregards a few sporadic attempts in the early 1680s, with the lavish production of *Dioclesian* at Dorset Garden in June 1690, more than a year after the premiere of *Dido*. *Dioclesian*, like all of Purcell's subsequent major stage works, is a semi-opera or "dramatick opera," that is, a five-act, spoken tragi-comedy with masques and entertainments sung by minor, often unnamed, characters. Many nineteenth- and twentieth-century commentators have regarded these large works as forming a corrupt sub-operatic genre on which Purcell squandered his genius. Through ignorance, they have failed to appreciate that on the whole, they include much finer music than *Dido*: longer-breathed melodies, more sophisticated harmony and counterpoint, and more richly developed characters. Not a shred of evidence has ever been produced to show that Purcell was dissatisfied with semi-opera or frustrated at not being able to follow *Dido* with another through-composed music drama.

Yet, among all of Purcell's works, only *Dido*, with its simple and diminutive airs, has a secure place in the modern repertory. The reasons are clear: it is self-contained, musically integrated, and overwhelmingly tragic, though Purcell's contemporaries apparently found the last aspect wholly unremarkable and, given the absence of violence, completely outside their experience in the theatre. In John Blow's *Venus and Adonis* (*c.* 1682), a masque for the private entertainment of King Charles II, Purcell found a model for almost everything in *Dido*: a three-act miniature opera with allegorical prologue; a chorus and *corps de ballet* essential to the action; an imperious though sympathetic queen-protagonist; a plastic style of recitative which was ideal for singing cramped English verse; and a basic dramatic structure derived ultimately from Lully's *tragédies en musique*. But *Venus and Adonis*, even though the hero dies in his lover's arms in the final scene, is not really tragic, because it lacks dramatic conflict at the purely human level. In this respect *Dido* is *sui generis* in the English Baroque.

For adapting Virgil's bitterly ironic account of Dido's suicide to suit Purcell's overriding desire to achieve a pathetic love-death without a trace of sentimentality, we have to thank the librettist Nahum Tate. He has been frequently attacked over the years for his choppy, unrhythmical verse and for occasional solecisms. Edward J. Dent described the libretto as "the most lamentable doggerel," and Sir Jack Westrup declared that as a poet Tate "deserves all the unkind things that have been said about him." (See p. 195.) But Westrup also appreciated the economy and balance of a libretto whose very irregularities in detail obviously appealed strongly to Purcell's manner of setting dramatic texts. It is high time that Tate's reputation as librettist and dramatist was repaired. Here is a synopsis of his deft rendering of the central episode of the fourth book of the *Aeneid*:

> *Act I.* After the Trojan wars, Prince Aeneas sets sail for Italy, where he is destined to refound the city of Troy on the banks of the Tiber. Blown off course by storms to the north coast of Africa, he is entertained by Dido, Queen of Carthage. Fascinated by the account of his heroic escape from the sack of Troy, she begins to fall in love with her guest, but, oppressed by the heavy affairs of state, is reluctant to yield completely. Urged on by her courtiers and especially by her cheerful confidante Belinda, she at length tacitly gives in to Aeneas, whose promise to postpone his departure for a passionate and indefinite sojourn in Carthage already sounds hollow, despite the formal rejoicing of the court at the prospect of a royal union.
>
> *Act II.* The scene changes to a cave, where the Sorceress, Dido's bitterest enemy, plots with a coven of witches to destroy Carthage by ruining the queen's amorous prospects. They plan to send an elf disguised as Mercury to Aeneas to remind him of his destiny, hoping that he will then abandon his royal lover. The second scene of this act is set in a grove, where Dido and Aeneas, having discreetly consummated their love the night before, are entertained by courtiers who perform songs and dances rich in hunting metaphors. With the outbreak of a violent storm conjured by the Sorceress, Dido and her followers rush back to town, while Aeneas stays behind to hear the message of the false Mercury: the elf proclaims that Jove himself has commanded the prince to waste no more time in love-

making. Amid loud and extravagant protestations, Aeneas precipitously resolves to set sail, as the witches reappear to gloat over the deceit.

Act III. In an ironic juxtaposition, the final act opens with Aeneas's sailors callously biding *their* "nymphs" farewell. The exultant Sorceress confidently predicts the queen's imminent death. At their last meeting the injured Dido despises Aeneas more for his cowardly promise to stay than for his concealed resolve to leave. She brusquely orders him away, but when he is gone realizes that she cannot live without him. With Belinda unable to console her, Dido dies (of a broken heart?). Cupids appear from the clouds and scatter roses on her tomb.

*   *   *

Dido was written for a fashionable boarding school in Chelsea (a leafy, Thames-side suburb west of London) where it was performed in spring 1689 by "Young Gentlewomen." Yet, in spite of the enormous popularity of his other stage music in the early 1690s, there is no record of a professional production of *Dido* until 1700, when, much altered, it was given as a series of four separate entertainments in an adaptation of *Measure for Measure*: Shakespeare's play was turned into a kind of semi-opera into which Purcell's music was more or less naturalistically introduced. Did the London audience shun *Dido* in its original form because they objected in principle to all-sung opera? If so, why was it not incorporated into a spoken play long before 1700? Did Purcell himself suppress it as one of his juvenilia? Did it have unfortunate political overtones which prevented a more public hearing during the reign of William and Mary (1689–95)? While none of these questions is easily answered, the writings assembled in this Critical Score clearly show that *Dido* was not only a musical foundling, in that it fitted into no operatic tradition or established genre, but that Tate and Purcell created a work that was politically and aesthetically out of step with the times.

Equally as vexing as the question of *Dido*'s initial reception are the problems surrounding its sources. To what extent is the earliest surviving score an accurate record of Purcell's lost original? The score in question, St. Michael's College, Tenbury, MS 1266 (5), which served as the basis for the edition reprinted in this volume, dates from after 1750 and differs significantly from the 1689 libretto and the text printed in Gildon's 1700 play-book: no music survives for either the lengthy prologue or the witches' chorus at the end of Act II. Whether this music has been lost or whether Purcell ever set these verses has long been the source of heated controversy. In this volume are assembled a number of essays—some of which are quite polemical—touching on both sides of the argument. While it may never be possible to prove or disprove that Purcell composed music for the prologue, the question of whether music is missing at the end of Act II will continue to be debated until a better score is found. As such a discovery now seems unlikely, the importance of the two librettos cannot be overestimated. They should probably take precedence over the Tenbury manuscript in almost all discrepancies of characterization, dramatic structure, and words. Considering the checkered performance history of the opera and the fact that, as Margaret Laurie shows, the Tenbury manuscript goes back to a production "no earlier than the third one," that is, 1704, we cannot say with certainty whether *Purcell* was responsible for any of the major deviations from the libretto, including the division of the opera into two instead of three parts. Every change must be examined individually by weighing the evidence of the various sources. To facilitate this process, I have included a critical edition of the libretto, which, for the first time, collates the three versions and reprints the prologue as well as the new scenes added by Gildon in 1700.

*   *   *

Opera is the most difficult kind of music to write about, and *Dido*, while of modest proportions, is no exception. Much of its literature is long on astonished admiration and short on genuine criticism, but this cannot be said of the excerpts presented below under the heading "Criticism and Analysis." They express strong opinions about the opera and occasionally bewail Purcell's fate never to have composed a more expansive sequel; but each writer examines the work's critical reception and analyzes its music strictly in terms of the drama. The informed reader will see at once that one important article is missing from the table of contents: the late Eric Walter White's "New Light on 'Dido and Aeneas'," which appeared in Imogen Holst's tercentenary volume dedicated to Purcell (1959). This is perhaps the most original essay on the opera since Dent's discussion in *Foundations of English Opera* (1928) (see p. 214). But White's ideas, unlike Dent's, have been so thoroughly absorbed by later writers (and quoted or referred to so often throughout this Critical Score) that reprinting the article in this context would have been a duplication.

I am grateful to Margaret Laurie, whose knowledge and understanding of *Dido* is second to none, for much help and advice and for agreeing to write what is in essence a new essay for this volume. Warm thanks also go to Jeremy Noble, Claire Brook, Roger Savage, and Richard Luckett for thoughtful suggestions about organization and contents, and to Michael Tilmouth for allowing his newly composed finale to Act II to be reprinted here.

HISTORICAL BACKGROUND

Dido and Aeneas *in Context*†

Virtually all that is known about the premiere of Purcell's *Dido and Aeneas* in the spring of 1689 is recorded on the first page of the libretto, probably printed for distribution to the audience.[1] It is by Nahum Tate, a minor playwright and tireless adapter of Shakespeare, who was to succeed Thomas Shadwell as poet laureate in 1692. The opera was given at a school run by Josias Priest, a choreographer at the Theatre Royal and, since the 1660s, an important dancer in the London playhouses. The only firm indication of the year of the premiere is Thomas Durfey's spoken epilogue, published in his *New Poems* in November 1689. The libretto states simply that the opera was performed "By Young Gentlewomen"; it sheds no light on who may have sung the part of Aeneas—if indeed it was intended for a man—not to mention the bass, tenor, and countertenor parts in the choruses. *Dido* was not the first such entertainment given at a school for girls in Chelsea. In 1676, Thomas Duffett and John Banister's *Beauties Triumph*, a half-spoken, half-sung dramatization of the Judgement of Paris, was acted at a "New Boarding-School for Young Ladies and Gentle-women" in the same house later occupied by Priest. The school masque may not have been an annual event at Chelsea, but both in and out of London spring musicals were probably commoner than records suggest.[2]

The most conspicuous precursor of *Dido and Aeneas* is Nahum Tate's tragedy *Brutus of Alba: or, The Enchanted Lovers* (1678), a thinly disguised retelling of the fourth book of the *Aeneid*. In the preface the author claims that he originally called the play "Dido and Aeneas," but on the advice of friends altered it to avoid his characters' being invidiously compared to Virgil's. Instead, he exhumed Geoffrey of Monmouth's contention in *Historia*

† Reprinted, with revisions and new material, from my book *Henry Purcell and the London Stage* (1984), by permission of Cambridge University Press.

1. The only copy is in the Royal College of Music, London. A facsimile is found in *The Works of Henry Purcell*, Vol. III, rev. Margaret Laurie (London: Novello, 1981), pp. xiii–xx.

2. See Neal Zaslaw, "An English 'Orpheus and Euridice' of 1697," *The Musical Times*, 118 (1977), 805–8.

Regum Britanniae that Brutus was Aeneas's great-grandson. The play finds the hero en route to conquer Albion, diverting to Syracuse to enact with its queen his great-grandfather's ill-fated affair with the queen of Carthage.[3] While the two works have essentially the same plot, the influence of *Brutus of Alba* on *Dido and Aeneas* is less than one might expect. *Brutus* is a full-blooded heroic play, a complex and fantastical fabrication centered on the classical conflict of love and honor, whereas *Dido* is pure opera, with simple but intense characters, from which all verbosity has been boiled away. The main persons represented in the two works do bear superficial resemblances:

Brutus	Aeneas
Queen of Syracuse	Dido, Queen of Carthage
Amarante, her confidante	Belinda
Ragusa, a sorceress	Sorceress

but to bolster an analysis of Purcell's characters with those of the play can lead to erroneous interpretations. First of all, the reasons for the catastrophe — Aeneas's abandonment of Dido and her subsequent death — are different. In *Brutus* the royal pair consummate their love under the influence of a potion administered by the sorceress. The queen's guilt at this sin is nonetheless acute and contributes to her fatal derangement. In *Dido* the consummation is ambiguous, and on the surface neither guilt nor madness is a major factor in the queen's death. As several writers have pointed out, the problem with the opera is Aeneas, who is little more than a glorified pawn in an evil game of magic. Joseph Kerman goes so far as to call him "a complete booby."[4] Aeneas deserts Dido because the Sorceress, motivated by an ill-defined hatred for the queen, tricks him into believing that Jove has commanded him to waste no more time "In Loves delights." In the play, however, Brutus's exit is agonizing and protracted. Asaracus, his boyhood friend and fellow warrior, is so sickened by the hero's dalliance with the Queen of Syracuse that he kills himself. Finally brought to his senses by this ultimate sacrifice, Brutus honors Asaracus's dying wish and sails away to Albion. Though Aeneas is the mere shadow of Brutus, both he and Dido are far more human than their counterparts in the play.

The most important musical precursor of *Dido* is John Blow's masque *Venus and Adonis*, which was performed about 1682 as a private entertainment for Charles II. Like Purcell's opera, it seems to have made little impres-

3. For a discussion of the links between the two legends, see below, pp. 228–35, and Robert R. Craven, "Nahum Tate's Third *Dido and Aeneas*: The Sources of the Libretto to Purcell's Opera," *The World of Opera*, 1 (1979), 65–78.
4. See the extract from *Opera as Drama*, reprinted below, p. 224.

sion, though it is hardly less a masterpiece. No part of the score was printed at the time, nor did it gain the composer a reputation in the theatre, if indeed the retiring Blow desired this kind of fame. Yet the selection in 1684 of the Spaniard Louis Grabu as composer for Dryden's through-composed opera *Albion and Albanius* must have been a slap in the face to all native theatre composers, including Blow, to judge by Dryden's touchy and defensive preface to the libretto. It might appear that in *Dido and Aeneas* Purcell was showing Dryden and the theatrical establishment a better way to write an English opera. But the two works are hardly comparable, and none of their contemporaries would have thought them to be of the same genre. Yet *Albion and Albanius*, which is a *tragédie en musique* in all but language, inevitably influenced Purcell. A model for *Dido*'s basic dramatic unit of recitative-air-chorus-dance could have been found in either Grabu's opera or in Lully's *Cadmus et Hermione*, which was performed in London in 1686. And the prologue to *Dido*, in which Phoebus, Venus, Spring, nymphs, shepherds, Tritons, and Nereids sing, is clearly reminiscent of *Albion and Albanius*, all the more so because both works were allegories designed to compliment the British monarchy.

Dido is not then, as some critics claim, the only example of a rare species, a single sprig of green in a opera-barren theatrical tradition. But why did it languish in total obscurity until 1698, when the protagonist's opening aria, "Ah! Belinda, I am press'd," appeared in the first book of the posthumous anthology *Orpheus Britannicus*, the only part of the score published before 1700? A school performance would not necessarily have meant oblivion: both the libretto and some of the songs of Thomas Duffett and John Banister's *Beauties Triumph* of 1676 were published after its suburban premiere, as was some of Richard Goodson and John Weldon's music for an *Orpheus and Euridice* given at a school near Oxford in 1697.[5] Nor was the English audience's failure to show an interest in a self-contained, all-sung music drama entirely responsible for the lack of a revival at the Theatre Royal during Purcell's lifetime. The work could have been presented as an afterpiece or entertainment in a play, as indeed it was in 1700 and 1704. The selection of "Ah! Belinda" for *Orpheus Britannicus* is hardly surprising, because it is the one substantial air in the opera without a built-in chorus. Even so, the concluding ritornel is omitted from the anthology, as are many such instrumental preludes and postludes.

Did the composer himself suppress the opera? Surely he could have made the adjustments necessary for the publication of excerpts, as he or his agents

---

5. See Zaslaw, op. cit.

did to *Dioclesian* and parts of *The Fairy-Queen* shortly after their premieres. The year 1690 seems to have been a watershed for Purcell. The editors of *Orpheus Britannicus*, who obviously had access to most of the composer's vocal music, decided to print very few songs known to have been written before 1690. Even after *Dido* made its professional debut in 1700, critics did not count it among the composer's great works. In 1710 Charles Gildon wrote: "Let any Master compare *Twice ten hundred Deities* [from *The Indian Queen*], the Music in the *Frost Scene* [in *King Arthur*], several Parts of the *Indian Queen*, and twenty more Pieces of *Henry Purcel*, with all the *Arrieto's, Dacapo's, Recitativo's* of *Camilla, Pyrrhus, Clotilda*, &c. and then judge which excels."[6] Eight years later, the same author, who was, as I explain below, intimately acquainted with *Dido*, repeated the opinion that the Frost Scene is a great achievement.[7] The absence of any mention of the opera in the writings of Roger North, Joseph Addison, and other early eighteenth-century writers on music does not necessarily imply that *Dido* was regarded as unworthy, only that other works, particularly parts of *King Arthur* and *The Indian Queen*, were considered far more impressive.

THE ALLEGORY

John Buttrey has argued that nearly all the major English operatic works of the period 1656–1695 were designed to compliment the monarchy if not the monarch. The clearest example is *Albion and Albanius*, which depicts the Restoration of Charles II in allegorical terms. Buttrey maintains that *Dido*, too, had an allegorical purpose that emerges when the work is viewed against the background of the first year of the reign of William and Mary.[8] In the prologue, Phoebus's glorious passage over the sea refers to William's expedition to England in 1688. And the descent of Venus, whose luster, Phoebus admits, "does out-shine / Your fainter beams, and half eclipses mine," obviously alludes to Mary II. These lines neatly express the unique division of the monarchy into king and queen regnant, whereby William administered the government in both their names. And the opera proper includes more than one reference to sharing the throne, as in the first-act chorus "When monarchs unite how happy their state, / They triumph at once o'er their foes and their fate." But a closer interpretation of the opera as allegory engenders a major problem. The story of a prince who seduces and abandons a neurotic queen would seem a tactless way to honor the new monarchs. Buttrey accounts for

6. *The Life of Mr. Thomas Betterton* (1710), p. 167.
7. *The Complete Art of Poetry* (1718), p. 103.
8. See below, pp. 228–35.

the apparent faux pas by viewing the opera as a cautionary tale; Tate dramatizes "the possible fate of the British nation should Dutch William fail in his responsibilities to his English queen . . . [the] choice of subject was apparently intended to reflect the political turbulence that must have been uppermost in many minds in 1689."[9] But even this charitable reading leads to unflattering parallels. Aeneas, legendary great-grandfather of Brutus the founder of Albion, leaves his beloved queen and sails across the sea to liberate a foreign land and establish a new kingdom. A cynic might therefore have seen in the Trojan prince William of Orange, the dour and reluctant hero, preparing to leave Holland for his destiny in England. But then Dido would symbolize Mary, a linkage that Tate surely wanted to avoid, cautionary tale or no.

Evidence that the story of Dido and Aeneas might have had unpleasant connotations during the reign of William and Mary is found in the dedication to Dryden's translation of the *Aeneid*. Though published in 1697, the project had occupied him for several years, and he even delayed its appearance in the vain hope that he would be able to lay it at the feet of a restored James II, to whom the poet remained loyal to the end. As has recently been shown, both the dedication (or introduction) and the translation itself contain a veiled attack on Elective Kingship, whereby Dryden invites parallels to be drawn between a rather unscrupulous Aeneas and William III, an inversion of Virgil's supposed intention that Aeneas be seen as a reflection of his king, Augustus Caesar.[10]

Dryden viewed Book IV in an especially cynical light. The entire episode in Carthage was invented, so he claims, primarily as a gloss on marriage and divorce: Dido regards the consummation in the cave as a marital act. In Dryden's words, "That the Ceremonies were short we may believe, for *Dido* was not only amorous, but a Widow. Mercury . . . owns it a Marriage by an *innuendo*. . . . He calls *Aeneas* not only a Husband, but upbraids him for being a fond Husband . . ."[11] Dryden claims that the reason Virgil so stretched this point — even created a two-hundred-year anachronism by making Dido and Aeneas contemporaries — was to prepare the way for "the Divorce which he intended afterwards," that is, to allow the Trojan prince to ridicule Dido's delusion that they were ever married, as an excuse for leaving her. Virgil thereby hoped to justify through allegory Augustus's divorce of his wife Scribonia. The political purpose of this elaborate design was to fan the flames of

9. See below, pp. 235.

10. See Steven N. Zwicker, *Politics and Language in Dryden's Poetry: the Arts of Disguise* (Princeton University Press, 1984), pp. 177-205.

11. *The Poems of John Dryden*, ed. James Kinsley (Oxford: Clarendon, 1958), Vol. III, lines 1131-5.

hatred for Carthage by attacking the reputation of the founder of Rome's great rival city.

Dryden offers only slim and contorted evidence for this bizarre interpretation. For example, he regards Mercury's aside about Dido, *varium &* *mutabile semper femina* (in essence, "women are fickle"), as "the sharpest Satire in the fewest words that was ever made on Womankind," because "varium" and "mutabile" are neuter rather than feminine; for this line to make sense, "animal" must therefore be understood (lines 1020-3). For whatever reason, Dryden never looks sympathetically on Dido. He admits that such virulent cynicism will not please his women readers, who would condemn Aeneas in forsaking Dido, but he coolly suggests that they "learn by experience at her cost; and for her sake; avoid a Cave, as the worst shelter they can chuse from a shower of Rain, especially when they have a Lover in their Company" (lines 878-80).

I would not imply that either Purcell or Tate shared the embittered Dryden's crotchety views of Virgil's Book IV (or that they were even opponents of William III), but this political reading of the *Aeneid* does illustrate that in the early 1690s the opera might have been regarded in some quarters as highly sensitive. Near the beginning of the dedication, Dryden provides just a hint that he disapproved of Purcell's venture. After observing that many plays which are good on the stage are inferior literature, he notes that there are also some "real Beauties in the reading" which would be absurd as dramas. For example, the "prowess of *Achilles* or *Aeneas*" would appear "ridiculous in our Dwarf-Heroes of the Theatre" and "cannot be represented even in Opera's . . ." (lines 191-6). If this is a veiled reference to Purcell's opera, then it is the only contemporary comment that the masterpiece elicited.[12]

Given that Book IV was likely to be misconstrued in the aftermath of the Bloodless Revolution, Tate was forced to adapt the classical tale, already deeply entwined with the supposed origins of the British monarchy, to disengage Queen Mary from a symbolic link with Queen Dido. This required major changes of plot, motivation, and characterization. I believe that the gaping ambiguities in the libretto—the reason for Dido's grief in Act I, the uncertain consummation of the couple's love in Act II, the enchantresses' unmotivated hatred of the queen, and even the manner of Dido's death—are owing directly to the potentially sensitive nature of the allegory. Had Tate followed Virgil as closely as in *Brutus of Alba*, faithfully depicting the queen's obsessive love for Aeneas, their winter of debauchery, her paralyzing guilt,

---

12. The two giants were well acquainted, having later collaborated on *Amphitryon* and *King Arthur* in 1690-1.

extreme bitterness, and blazing anger at his departure, eyebrows would have been raised from Chelsea to Whitehall.

A radical alteration of the basic structure of Virgil's account of the Queen of Carthage is the introduction of the Sorceress and her witches, or, to be precise, her enchantresses, since Tate never calls them witches in the 1689 libretto. They provide the catalyst for the tragedy, but their hatred of Dido is not explained. A desire to "share in the Fame / Of a Mischief" is their only motivation. They have long troubled critics because, in stark contrast to Dido, the witches lack human emotions.[13] Of course, they symbolize "the malevolence of destiny," as Jack Westrup remarks.[14] The Sorceress herself makes this clear: "The *Trojan* Prince you know is bound / By Fate to seek *Italian* Ground" (II.i). She is simply hastening Aeneas's inevitable departure from Carthage, while vowing the queen's destruction. Ragusa, the sorceress in *Brutus of Alba*, plays a tangential role in the queen's death, being only a soothsayer and plotter against the government. But her counterpart in *Dido* is "almost as impressive a figure as Dido herself,"[15] an antagonist whose malignity is highly developed. Indeed, one could argue that the villainess represents not "the gods of destiny" but the dark side of the queen. Roger Savage even proposes that the scenes for the witches are a "black parody" from which the "sentiments and rituals of the court can be grotesquely guyed..."[16]

Though Edward J. Dent viewed the introduction of the witches as highly implausible, he acquitted Tate of the charge that their appearance should have been better justified: "one might imagine that Restoration audiences could not conceive of an opera without them."[17] He is of course alluding to Davenant's 1663–4 version of *Macbeth*, whose scenes for Heccate and the witches, expanded from Shakespeare and set to music by Locke, Eccles, and Leveridge at various times during the period, are widely acknowledged as a major source for Tate's enchantresses.[18] The members of both covens are called "weyward sisters," and they express their "motiveless malignity" in similar terms, as shown in the following examples:

---

13. See below for the comments of Robert E. Moore, p. 223 and Edward Dent, p. 216.
14. See below, p. 196.
15. See Moore, *Henry Purcell*, p. 52.
16. See below, p. 265.
17. *Foundations of English Opera* (1928; Reprint. New York: Da Capo, 1965), p. 185.
18. See *Five Restoration Adaptations of Shakespeare*, ed. Christopher Spencer (Urbana: University of Illinois Press, 1965), pp. 14–16. Dent exaggerates the role of witches in the drama of the time. Cauldron-stirring hags of the sort depicted by Middleton, Shakespeare, and Davenant are rare in both plays and semi-operas.

Davenant	*Tate*
To us fair weather's foul, and foul is fair (I.i)	Destruction's our delight, delight our greatest Sorrow (III)
We shou'd rejoyce when good Kings bleed (II.v)	From the ruin of others our pleasures we borrow,
	Elisa bleeds to Night . . . (III)
Have I not reason *Beldams*? (III.viii)	Say *Beldam* what's thy will? (II.i)
But whilst she moves through the foggy Air,	In our deep Vaulted Cell the Charm wee'l prepare,
Let's to the Cave and our dire Charms prepare (III.viii)	Too dreadful a Practice for this open Air (II.i)

But these are only superficial resemblances. In Davenant, the witches' chief functions are to prophesy the bloody succession from Duncan to Macbeth and to add scenic and musical spectacle. Ludicrously overdrawn to symbolize the protagonists' malevolent ambition, they are, paradoxically, crucial to the action and dramatically redundant. The enchantresses in *Dido* play quite a different role. They both prophesy and cause catastrophic events.

An equally important source for the witches of the opera are the earthy crones in Thomas Shadwell's strange and very popular play *The Lancashire Witches* (1681), a savage satire on Roman Catholicism, embodied in the vile Irish priest Tegue O Divelly and the meddling chaplain Smerk. In the years following the Popish Plot (c. 1678–80) when the succession of the Catholic Duke of York became increasingly likely, attacks on religion carried strong political implications, and several scenes of the sub-plot were duly cut or drastically shortened by the Master of the Revels. The most notorious scenes in the play involve the witches, unabashedly introduced to exploit the musical and mechanical advantages of the Dorset Garden theatre. The prompter John Downes even describes the play as "a kind of Opera, having several *Machines* of Flyings for the Witches. . . ."[19] Shadwell acknowledges a debt to Shakespeare (actually Davenant) but stresses that unlike the witches in *Macbeth*, which he incorrectly believed to have been created entirely from the bard's imagination, his wayward sisters are based "from Authority" on real people. In notes appended to the end of each act, he documents their ritualistic cant and weird behavior with voluminous references to various writings on witchcraft. The leader, Mother Demdike, is a model for the Sorceress in *Dido*, especially in her unmotivated evil-doing. Tate seems to have taken the idea for the storm that ruins Dido and Aeneas's hunting party from Shadwell. Mother Demdike spoils the hare-coursing in Act I with mischievous magic,

19. *Roscius Anglicanus* (1707), ed. Montague Summers (London: Fortune, [1928]), p. 38.

then conjures up a spectacular tempest. Tate's enchantresses even speak like Shadwell's witches. For example, in II.ii of the opera the bogus Mercury sings "To Night thou must forsake this Land, / The Angry God will brook no longer stay," an echo of Mother Demdike's "Come, Sisters, come why do you stay? / Our business will not brook delay" (I.i). But Tate's greatest debt to Shadwell is the Sorceress's air of not-quite-human glee at her misdeeds.

Tracing the sources of the enchantresses in *Dido* does not, however, explain their important role. In *Macbeth*, the witches are the postilions of an inevitable train of events. In *Brutus of Alba*, their malevolence is spectacular though of little effect. And in *The Lancashire Witches*, they themselves become the tragic victims of superstition, prejudice, and a kangaroo court. Shadwell's play nevertheless holds the key to the virulent role of the Sorceress in *Dido*. Though the playwright's announced purpose for including the witches was "to make as good an entertainment as I could, without tying my self up to the strict rules of a Comedy" (from the preface), he also intended their mystical and altogether distasteful ceremonies to satirize Catholic ritual. By the fourth act, there is little difference between the inquisitor Tegue and the victim, Mother Demdike. Of the priest, the cynical Lady Shacklehead remarks, "I do not know what to think of his Popish way, his Words, his Charms, and Holy water, and Relicks, methinks he is guilty of Witchcraft too, and you should send him to Gaol for it." Thus averting the censor's heavy hand, Shadwell makes the witches represent the Catholic clergy.

An allegorical purpose of the enchantresses in *Dido* can now be postulated. The greatest threat to the stability of the English monarchy in 1689 was the restoration of James II and the attendant resurgence of popery. In the opera the destruction of love between Dido and Aeneas and therewith any hope of a joint reign is accomplished by cheap magic. Considering the close connection between the wayward sisters and Roman Catholicism in Shadwell's *The Lancashire Witches* and the strong influence of Mother Demdike on the Sorceress, one must conclude that the witches in *Dido* symbolize a new popish plot, as mindless as the original one of 1678 but still with potentially fatal consequences.[20] This interpretation, however repugnant, best explains why Tate replaced Virgil's "cruel fate" and his own love-and-honor conflict in *Brutus of Alba* with the Sorceress's ritualistic evil as the engine of tragedy.

Although Tate is faithful to his source in depicting Dido as a woman wronged in love, he eliminates virtually any trace of the *Aeneid*'s preoccupation with her sexual indulgence and subsequent guilt. To attribute the omis-

---

20. The hypothesis is closely paralleled in Mary Chan, "The Witch of Endor and Seventeenth-Century Propaganda," *Musica Disciplina*, 34 (1980), 205-14.

sions, simplifications, and obfuscations of Virgil's detailed account of her psychopathy solely to the epigrammatic brevity of the libretto and the tender age of the performers is a naive interpretation. Having chosen a story with potential application to Queen Mary, Tate is forced to suppress Dido's faults in favor of a noble, almost austere righteousness. This compromise is felt most acutely in Act I. The queen refuses to reveal the cause of her melancholy ("I am prest, / With Torment not to be Confest"). Nearly all writers on the opera have assumed that she, like Virgil's Dido, is sufferir g "the anguish of love." Moore, for example, describes her as "love-sick," "perplexed," and reluctant "to yield to love."[21] Tate makes no reference to the cause of her anxiety: Virgil's queen is in mourning for her late husband, Sychaeus, in whose memory she has taken a pledge of chastity; but she has also developed an overpowering attraction for Aeneas. Perhaps Tate omitted to mention this conflict in order to avoid showing how easily Dido forgets her solemn vow to the dead king. At all events, her affliction seems more a neurosis than a heroic dilemma, as if the librettist were still tied to the necromantic Queen of Syracuse in *Brutus of Alba*, who remains physically married to her dead husband (called Argaces), spending each night in his tomb, sometimes in the company of his ghost. Her existence is a living death, certainly an allusion to be kept out of the minds of the 1689 audience. Of course, Dido should not be burdened with baggage from the earlier play, but mere widowhood does not adequately explain her stubborn resistance to Aeneas's courtship and then her silent submission. As is shown below, Tate's attempt to rid his protagonist of the flaws so vividly described by Virgil caused more problems than it solved.

MEASURE FOR MEASURE

After Purcell's death in November 1695, all his semi-operas and plays with music apparently remained the property of the Theatre Royal, Drury Lane.[22] During the next eleven years of intense competition between the old company and Thomas Betterton's new theatre in Lincoln's Inn Fields (a rivalry that ended with a sweeping reorganization of the London playhouses in 1706), the Theatre Royal repeatedly revived all Purcell's major stage works except *The Fairy-Queen*, the score of which was lost shortly after the composer's death. But while the company was milking the music of "the late Mr. Purcell" for all it was worth, *Dido and Aeneas* was nowhere to be seen, which would seem to

---

21. *Henry Purcell & the Restoration Theatre* (Cambridge, Mass.: Harvard University Press, 1961), p. 41.

22. Though no document allocating repertory to the two companies exists, such a separation of musical works composed before spring 1695 can be deduced from a survey of performance records.

indicate that the theatre did not possess a copy. Early in 1700 the opera finally made its professional debut as a series of masques in Charles Gildon's adaptation of *Measure for Measure*, given not at Drury Lane but at Lincoln's Inn Fields. *Dido* is, then, Purcell's only major stage work for which Betterton was able to obtain the rights. The 1700 production is of utmost importance in understanding how the composer's near contemporaries interpreted the opera and why the surviving score is only a fragment of the original.

In his analysis of how the opera was altered when conjoined with the play, Eric Walter White noted that *Dido* was not merely "given as an interlude," as Alfred Loewenberg had maintained, but that *Measure for Measure* was itself considerably changed to accommodate the music.[23] The stated rationale for the "play"-within-the-play is to sweeten Angelo's "Sour Temper." In the absence of the duke, his deputy Angelo has priggishly resurrected an old statute against fornication. First to be condemned for infringing it is the worthy Claudio. Escalus, Angelo's chief minister, who believes in tempering justice with mercy, has arranged a performance of the little opera as an apologue to show Angelo the possible consequences of enforcing too zealously a law against nature. Aeneas is thus meant to represent Claudio, and Dido the violated Julietta. The allegory implies an interpretation of the central ambiguity of *Dido and Aeneas* in direct opposition to almost all modern criticism: in the new context, the lovers have committed a sin punished by the havoc wrought when the Sorceress tricks Aeneas into abandoning the queen. Angelo acknowledges the design, but instead of being morally instructed or even moved by the tragedy, he sees *himself* as Aeneas, an anti-heroic perversion of Virgil's protagonist.

In Act I, scene i Lucio explains that the opera will be heard in four separate parts in order not to tire Angelo with too much music at once. Shortly before the first entertainment, which is placed near the end of Act I, Claudio's sister, the virtuous Isabella, appeals to Angelo to pardon her brother for his crime. The deputy says he will consider her suit when "the Opera is over." As in Shakespeare, he is smitten by her beauty, but Gildon abridges the memorable soliloquy through which Angelo's hypocrisy begins to surface (Shakespeare, II.ii.162–86) and supplies a transition to the first act of *Dido*:

> I'll think no more on't, but with Musick chase
> Away the Guilty Image.
> Musick they say can Calm the ruffled Soul,
> I'm sure a mighty Tempest ruffles mine.

---

23. "New Light on 'Dido and Aeneas'," in *Henry Purcell, 1659–1695*, ed. Imogen Holst (London: Oxford University Press, 1959), pp. 14–34.

Instead of quelling his lust, the masque fans the flames. After the first act, he
says:

> This Musick is no Cure for my Distemper;
> For, every Note, to my Enchanted Ears,
> Seem'd to Sing only *Isabella*'s Beauty,
> Her Youth, her Beauty, and her Tender Pity
> Combine to ruin me! Ha! Dost thou then
> Desire her foully?

The next act of the opera is presented after the second interview (II.ii),
in which Angelo tells Isabella that her brother will be spared if she will submit
to his desire. While mulling over her refusal to acquiesce, he listens to the
scenes in which the Sorceress plots Dido's destruction, a storm spoils the hunting party, and the spirit *"in likeness* of Mercury" commands Aeneas to leave
the queen and sail on to his destiny. Angelo twists the masque into a grotesque
metaphor of his designs on Isabella:

> All will not do: All won't devert my Pain,
> The Wound enlarges by these Medicines,
> 'Tis She alone can yield the Healing Balm.
> This Scene just hits my case; her Brothers danger,
> Is here the storm must furnish Blest Occasion;
> And when, my Dido, I've Possess'd thy Charms,
> I then will throw thee from my glutted Arms,
> And think no more on all thy soothing Harms.

Note that he reads far more into the second act of the opera than the elliptic
plot suggests, comparing Claudio's death sentence for fornication, and the
leverage it gives him with Isabella, to the tempest that offers Dido the "Blest
Occasion" for satisfying her lust. But according to Tate's 1689 libretto, Aeneas
has already "enjoy'd" one night *before* the storm scatters the hunting party.
By hammering home this allegory, Gildon exploits the very aspect of the
Aeneid that Tate attempted to obscure. When one strips Book IV of the inter-
ference of the gods, the cause of the human tragedy is that Dido regards her
submission in the cave during the storm as tantamount to marriage, whereas
Aeneas does not. In the memorable words of Dryden's verse translation,

> The queen, whom sense of honour could not move,
> No longer made a secret of her love,
> But called it marriage; by that specious name
> To veil the crime, and sanctify the shame.

But Aeneas later tells her that he never "pretended to the lawful claim / Of
sacred nuptials, or a husband's name," which applies directly to Angelo's
seduction and abandonment of Mariana before the play began. The opera

thus emphasizes the monstrousness of the hypocrisy in condemning Claudio for violating the sacred vow of marriage.

The third act of the opera is placed in Act III, scene ii. Escalus tells Angelo that the final entertainment will "compose your Thoughts for pleasing Slumbers." But the villain is distracted throughout the performance, because he expects Isabella, who has promised to meet him at this hour, to appear. Delaying her entrance until just before the end of the opera is a brilliant touch: as Dido dies of shame (at least in Angelo's mind), Isabella seems ready to offer up her virginity. Unmoved by the great musical tragedy just acted before him, he mutters malevolently, "I see my Ev'ning Star of Love appear." Purists may view the joining of opera and play as a misguided conflation that saps the lifeblood from each, but I think the union helped to resolve, if only temporarily, the troublesome ambiguities surrounding Aeneas. When the allegorical links to William III are severed, the Trojan prince emerges as the hypocritical opportunist of Dido's dying accusations. Gildon's adaptation removes Purcell's opera from its pedestal of royal panegyric, transforming it into a story of intense human passions. Dido's love for Aeneas is a *carpe diem*, not just in the literal sense, but also in the Freudian: an immoral sexual liaison for which she must ultimately pay.

THE LIBRETTOS AND THE TENBURY SCORE

The earliest score of *Dido and Aeneas*, Tenbury MS 1266 (5) (now in the Bodleian Library, Oxford), dates from more than fifty years after the premiere and disagrees with Tate's 1689 libretto in two significant ways: it lacks the French-style allegorical prologue and the chorus "Then since our Charms have Sped" at the end of Act II. The differences between the manuscript and the libretto have long troubled scholars. If Purcell originally set the prologue and verse at the end of Act II, why are they not preserved in Tenbury? Does the score in fact bear any resemblance to the one used for the Chelsea premiere, or is it thoroughly corrupt both in detail and general dramatic outline, like many mid-eighteenth-century manuscripts of Purcell's other stage works? To answer these questions one must start with the librettos.

Though the opera text printed in the 1700 version of *Measure for Measure* corrects many misprints and freely alters Tate's stage directions, it is clear that Gildon and his printer worked from a copy of the 1689 libretto.[24] Yet the order of acts and scenes is radically different:

---

24. See the notes to the critical edition given below, pp. 63ff, esp. Act III, no. 11.

	1689 libretto		*1700 libretto*
Prologue		Act I	The Palace
i	Phoebus, Venus, et al.	Act II.ii	The Grove [expanded]
ii	Spring	II.i	The Sorceress's Cave
iii	Shepherds	Act III	The Ships
Act I	The Palace	Prologue	
Act II.i	The Sorceress's Cave	i	Phoebus, Venus, et al.
II.ii	The Grove		[Spring omitted]
Act III	The Ships	ii	Shepherds
		iii	Mars, Peace [new scene]

The prologue is placed at the end of the play to serve as a celebration of the duke's Solomonic wisdom in preserving Isabella's chastity and Claudio's life. As an introduction, this scene, which is entirely separate from the opera itself, would have obscured the allegory. As a final entertainment, it had to be provided with a vacuous new ending—a debate between Mars and Peace—which displaced the entry of Spring and advanced the original dialogue for a shepherd and shepherdess into second position.

The reversal of the order of scenes in Act II is illogical, because in the 1700 version the Sorceress's declaration that her "elf" shall appear to Aeneas in the form of Mercury is made after the event. White's explanation of the transposition is as good as any: rearranging the scenes allowed the second part of the opera to end with the only spectacular machine effects in the play.[25] After the Echo Dance, six furies sink below the stage and four others fly up. The furies seem to have been Gildon's invention, because Tate's libretto, which requires no machine effects in this scene, calls for a dance of "*Inchanteresses and Fairees.*" But exigencies of staging would not appear to account wholly for the radical change in the order of events in the opera, especially considering how carefully Gildon exploits the allegorical connections between the two works. As noted above, Angelo misreads events depicted in the opera when he likens the storm to the death sentence imposed on Isabella's brother. The transposition of scenes in Act II may therefore be a clumsy attempt to relate the opera more closely to the play, by allowing Angelo to reason that he and Isabella, like Dido and Aeneas, have not yet had the "Blest Occasion." This sequence would also mirror Tate's *Brutus of Alba*, in which the episode at Diana's fountain (the Grove scene in the opera) occurs *before* the consummation.

This may be giving Gildon more credit than he deserves, but the other major alteration of Act II clearly underscores the parallel between opera and

25. "New Light on 'Dido and Aeneas'," pp. 23–4.

play. After the bogus Mercury delivers the fateful message to Aeneas, Gildon inserted a twenty-four-line dialogue for two friends of the hero, who debate what course he should take.[26] One counsels him to follow the dictates of his heart and remain with Dido, while the other reminds him of the greater rewards of fame and glory. Aeneas has already resolved to leave ("Yours be the blame, ye Gods, for I / Obey you will—but with more Ease cou'd dye"), but after hearing his friends' conflicting advice he wavers: "Ye Sacred Powers instruct me how to choose, / When Love or Empire I must loose." This is a blatant reference to Angelo's crisis of conscience. No music survives for these added verses, but they were probably set by John Eccles, Lincoln's Inn Fields's chief composer, since he is known to have provided the incidental music for the 1700 production of *Measure for Measure*.[27]

The Tenbury manuscript restores the scenes in Act II to their original sequence, while omitting Gildon's debate between Aeneas's friends, and is therefore closer to the original libretto than to the one printed in the *Measure for Measure* quarto. Placing great faith in a score copied more than sixty years after the event and ignoring the contrary evidence provided by the librettos, Dent maintained that Purcell did not set the prologue, and if he did, "it is no great loss."[28] He also thought the composer cut the chorus at the end of the Grove scene, "feeling that the despair of Aeneas made a more dramatic end to the act." Recently a more cogent argument has been advanced that Tenbury, "except perhaps for the missing Prologue, reflects Purcell's original intentions."[29] Yet, while the questions surrounding the prologue will probably never be resolved, most musicians who have performed and studied *Dido* conclude that the chorus and dance at the end of Act II are indeed lost. The gap is clearly shown by the overall tonal plan, which is beautifully balanced:

Acts	Principal key centers			
I	c	C	(e)	C
II.i	f	F	(d)	F
II.ii	d	D	(a)	—
III	B♭	g	(c)	g

26. Reprinted below with the libretto on pp. 78–79. The dialogue may have been suggested by Aeneas's conference with the shipfitters Mnestheus, Sergestus, and Serestus, the *Aeneid*, IV. 288–91. Craven, in "Nahum Tate's Third *Dido and Aeneas*," p. 72, argues that the added lines, because of their supposed links to *Brutus of Alba*, were cut from the 1689 performance, but his evidence is inconclusive.

27. See Richard Charteris, "Some Manuscript Discoveries of Henry Purcell and His Contemporaries in the Newberry Library, Chicago," *Notes*, 37 (1980), 8–9.

28. *Foundations of English Opera*, p. 180.

29. Ellen T. Harris, *Handel and the Pastoral Tradition* (London: Oxford University Press, 1979), reprinted below, p. 251.

The first two scenes begin in minor keys and end in the parallel major. The third act opens in the major and concludes in the relative minor. Each main section includes at least one important piece in a key that temporarily disrupts the scheme: in Act I the E-minor chorus "Cupid only throws the dart" (No. 9);[30] in II.i the D-minor duet "But ere we this perform" (No. 20); and in Act III the recitative "Thy hand, Belinda" (No. 37), which begins in C minor and modulates back to G minor. The second scene of Act II begins like the preceding ones in a minor key and then shifts to the parallel major, but ends with an A-minor recitative that leaves the act dangling in a different key from the one in which it began. Furthermore, the formal chain of air (or duet), chorus, and dance that terminates all the other scenes is broken here. Many editors and directors have felt the need to insert music in D minor or D major to complete the act.[31]

How was this music lost? Let us hypothesize that Purcell set Tate's 1689 libretto virtually as it stands, changing a word here and there, dividing a few choruses into solos and ensembles, giving some of the Sorceress's couplets to the enchantresses, and strengthening Belinda's part by transferring a line or two from Dido—the kinds of alterations that opera composers from Monteverdi on made to their librettos as a matter of course. After its premiere, the score was put away and forgotten until Purcell's widow made his papers available to the editors of *Orpheus Britannicus*, who extracted only one aria from the opera. A year or two later, Betterton acquired the manuscript and probably paid Eccles to adapt it for *Measure for Measure*. The composer set the additional verses sandwiched between Aeneas's soliloquy and the witches' chorus in Act II and wrote a grand finale for the prologue. *Dido* proved successful enough to be revived in January 1704, when it was attached to Edward Ravenscroft's three-act farce *The Anatomist*, a popular play that incorporated Peter Motteux's masque *The Loves of Mars and Venus* (first produced in November 1696, with music by Eccles and Godfrey Finger). *Dido* was also added to a revival of Etherege's *The Man of Mode* later in 1704. Even if this play was presented in a moderately abridged form, the inclusion of the expanded version of *Dido* must have made for a very long evening. The opera

---

30. This and the numbers cited below refer to the rehearsal numbers in the present score.

31. See below, p. 183, for Michael Tilmouth's newly-composed finale for Act II. In Benjamin Britten and Imogen Holst's reconstruction (London: Boosey & Hawkes, 1961), the first half of the chorus is in D minor (a reworking and transposition from C minor of "What flatt'ring noise is this" from *The Indian Queen*), then shifts to D major for "A dance that shall make the spheres to wonder . . ." (based on "To Urania and Caesar" from the 1687 Birthday Song for James II, originally in C major), returning to D minor for the Groves dance (the canzona from the overture for *Sir Anthony Love*).

was probably stripped of the prologue for one of these performances. Further-more, I suspect that the editor for the 1704 revivals, knowing that in 1700 new music had been added after Aeneas's monody in the second act, lopped off the end of the scene at that point, unaware that he was also removing Purcell's original setting of the witches' chorus that followed the interpolated dialogue. Therefore, a well-intentioned attempt to purge the opera of music it had acquired when joined to *Measure for Measure* may explain the apparent gap at the end of Act II. The Tenbury score was, then, almost certainly based on a manuscript at least three stages removed from Purcell's original.

But Tenbury shows many signs of having been copied from an early manuscript, one used for a theatrical rather than a concert performance. For-tunately, the copyist made practically no attempt to modernize its antiquated notation: the viola part is in the mezzo-soprano clef; the key signatures of C minor and F minor mostly omit the flats on the sixth degree of the scale; except in two instances discussed below, sharps and flats rather than natural signs are used to cancel accidentals;[32] and accidentals are not necessarily can-celled by the bar-line. Perhaps the best clue to the date of Tenbury's source is the minimal bass figuring, which is limited to essentials. Continuo figuring was undergoing significant change about the time Purcell died. For example, *Orpheus Britannicus* (1698) is profusely figured in comparison to the pre-1695 prints from which most of its contents were copied. Purcell's own figur-ing in the few extant autographs of theatre music is also very simple, often petering out altogether after a line or two. In view of the many archaic fea-tures of the notation, I should guess that Tenbury was copied from a manu-script dating from about 1700.

Given his literal-mindedness, the scribe may have signalled some of his own tiny changes in the first act. The only natural signs of the entire score are those shown in Example 1, from the arietta for the "second woman." By using the new-fangled device here, the scribe may have wanted to show that the accidentals in the bass at bars 1 and 5 were not in his source and are thus edi-torial (note the "B♯" in bars 7 and 8). All modern editions include them be-cause they make a strong progression. But one must remember that *Dido* is an early work and such harmonic "irregularities" are not uncommon in Purcell's pre-1690 music.

The key of C minor, in which the opera begins, causes problems for edi-tors of late seventeenth-century music, because the signature normally has only two flats. A careful copyist, such as Purcell, overcame potential ambi-guity by indicating the A♭'s individually. But other scribes, in fact the large

---

32. The natural sign came into common use in England after 1710.

Example 1   "The greatest blessing fate can give," bars 1–9 as in Tenbury MS

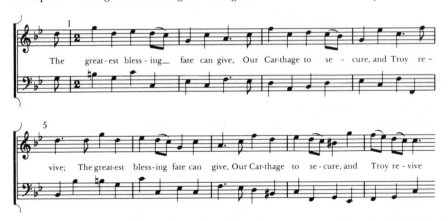

majority, relied on the performer to supply the appropriate sixth degree and even the sharp on the seventh according to the melodic direction and harmonic context. An editor must proceed warily; adding accidentals creates a more tonal, minor-key idiom that might be anachronistic. The Tenbury scribe was aware of this danger. He starts the score boldly with a two-flat signature for the C minor overture and Belinda's first air, writing in the A♭'s while leaving the A♮'s unsigned. But at the first chorus, "Banish sorrow, banish care," he mixes the modern three-flat signature with the old seventeenth-century notation. Dido's aria "Ah! Belinda" (No. 3) and the following recitative, both in C minor, return to two flats. The next chorus, "When monarchs unite" (No. 5), appears to have been written out initially in the old style, but an A♭ was later added to the key signature, perhaps in a different hand. Should the chords marked with asterisks in Example 2 have A♭ or A♮? Of course, we are used to hearing this piece with every A flatted, but the only unequivocal A♭ of the chorus is in bar 7. To sing all the others as A♮ produces

Example 2   "When monarchs unite"

(especially in bar 11) a distinctly modal sound not inconsistent with Purcell's early choral music. The Tenbury copyist endeavored to reconcile the fluid tonal style of *Dido* with his mid-eighteenth-century notation, happily accomplishing this without eradicating the archaisms of his source. He must have been an antiquary of rare musical sensitivity.

Such attention to detail does not suggest the sort of person who would have omitted sections from his source. Although he worked from an early manuscript, it was probably mutilated, already lacking the prologue and chorus at the end of Act II. Furthermore, the scenes are grouped differently from the 1689 libretto and in a manner inconsistent with the *Measure for Measure* play-book:

	1689 libretto	*Tenbury score*
Palace	I	I.i
Cave	II.i	I.ii
Grove	II.ii	II
Ships	III	III

The manuscript thus has a long first act and a rather short second one, an imbalance exaggerated by the missing witches' chorus. Margaret Laurie, the editor of the revised Purcell Society score reprinted in this volume, elected to retain the more logical format of Tate's libretto.[33]

33. For a further discussion of the disposition of scenes in the manuscript, see below, pp. 49-52.

MUSIC AND DRAMA

The correspondences between Blow's court masque *Venus and Adonis* and
the similarly proportioned *Dido and Aeneas* are too numerous to be coincidental. Each is an all-sung three-act miniature tragedy with a French-style
prologue, in which an imperious woman loses her lover. And the works share
a number of musical and structural features, including a carefully balanced
tonal plan centering on G minor, pervasive descending chromatics to depict
both grief and impending doom, moments of comic and pastoral relief, and a
final reflective chorus. The main dramatic difference between the operas is,
of course, that Adonis's death is accidental, whereas Dido's is the result of
human frailty and conflict. Like all great tragedians, Purcell avoids sentimen-
talism by accentuating the irony of the fatal catastrophe. But this too he may
have learned from Blow. The anonymous libretto for *Venus and Adonis* com-
pensates for a lack of impellent conflict by exaggerating the hackneyed irony
of the familiar story: Adonis wants to die metaphorically upon Venus's breast,
is diverted by the hunt and wounded by a boar, then dies in earnest in the
final scene. This is not unlike the main human action of the fourth book of
the *Aeneid*, though without the moralistic retribution. Virgil achieves a
fusion of sex and death by having Dido stab herself with Aeneas's sword, then
die on the bed in which they consummated their love. While Tate purged his
libretto of such explicit imagery, he did allude to the parallel theme of *Venus
and Adonis*. In the scene in the grove after Dido has succumbed to desire,
Aeneas boasts of his hunting prowess by displaying on the end of his spear a
"Monster's Head," presumably that of the elusive wild boar mentioned in the
Aeneid, IV. 159. A phallic symbol if ever there was one, this refers both to
Dido's "specious marriage" and to Adonis's fatal hunt. Aeneas even mentions
his mother at this point, remarking that the boar's tusks are larger than
"Those did Venus' Huntsmen tear," a linkage that foreshadows the disastrous
result of the royal pair's illicit union. Dido's response, "The Skies are Clouded,"
a panicky *non sequitur*, is as much a reaction to the sudden reminder of her
sin as it is to the gathering clouds conjured by the Sorceress. It is remarkable
how often *Dido and Aeneas* relies on *Venus and Adonis*, both literally and
figuratively, at important moments such as this.

Whereas Blow's masque may have provided Purcell with the basic in-
gredients of musical tragedy and allowed him to express metaphorically what
he dared not say openly, it did not furnish a model for the most compelling
feature of the opera: Dido is consumed from within rather than destroyed by
circumstances imposed by fate or perfidy. Hers is not a fall from grace, but a
progress from anguish, through guilt and rage, to morbid resignation. The
entire opera is a relentless descent to the grave, in which the Lament is the

4 "Ah! Belinda," bars 40-4

motif is the same as the ground's. Of the many masterstrokes, perhaps
most noteworthy is the recapitulation of the principal melody in bar 48
the modulation to G minor; the bass has unobtrusively returned to C
r a full eleven bars earlier. Despite such technical feats, the music re-
s expressive, as when Dido touches on the royal key, then shuns it with a
ncholy downward slide (Example 4). Purcell's characterization of the
ished queen is also conveyed by the low range of this aria.[34] This perhaps
ints for the *Orpheus Britannicus* editor's decision to transpose it up a
to D minor.
The recitatives and ariosos, about which much has been written, seem to
no more "heaven-sent" than the declamatory sections of many of the songs
dialogues in the rest of Purcell's dramatic music. But they are celebrated
use, for once, the singers are protagonists rather than decorative nymphs
shepherds. The recitatives in the first act are especially interesting, being
battleground for Dido's struggle of conscience. The exchange shown in
mple 5 is the most important, revealing a decided shift in the queen's
or as the music clarifies the most obscure couplets of the libretto. Dido's
estions are rhetorical, since presumably she has already been entertained
Aeneas's recounting his heroic exploits (the *Aeneid*, Books II and III).
rdan Anchises is of course his father, Venus his mother. Belinda's woeful
le is therefore the trail of tears the prince has followed since the sack of
roy. The recitative begins with bombast appropriate to storms and battles.
o depict Aeneas's inherited virtues, Dido sings alternately in C major (often
war key for Purcell) and F major (a love key). Belinda's response (bars 9-12),
hich, like the queen's preceding air on a ground, begins in C minor and
nodulates to G minor, gently chides Dido for her extravagant display of grief;
he upward slide on the word "woe" (bar 11) is especially mocking. Confirma-
ion that the queen has finally succumbed to her courtiers' exhortations comes

34. In general, Dido's range in the rest of the opera is that of a modern mezzo-soprano but
with a high tessitura.

Example

inevitable goal of a grand musical scheme. Al
the final aria; even the seemingly care-free mu
and the sailors' quay-side jollity at the beginnin
forebodings of tragedy.

The tonal scheme, a constellation of keys cl
paragon of simplicity. (See above, p. 17.) Its chi
story swiftly and to emphasize almost to the point
ing irony. The first two scenes have the same desig
minor key and end exuberantly in the parallel n
C-minor anguish is followed by her courtiers' celel
amorous alliance with Aeneas; in the second scen
incantation in F minor is succeeded by the enchant
in the parallel major over their forthcoming mischief.
scene of Act II, which begins in D minor, would repli
ing finale were recovered. The pattern is reversed in
sailors unknowingly join the witches in a swaggering I
impending G-minor tableau.

head
the m
after
mino
main
mela
angu
acco
tone

Example 3   Bass of Overture, bars 1-13

me
and
bec
and
the
Ex
do
qu
by
D
ta
T
T
a
v
r
t

The French overture (No. 1) plunges directly into tl
over Dido's court. The first section writhes with a chron
seems to lead nowhere; the tortuous descent of the bass after
pedal (see Example 3) graphically points the drama on its wa
sant eighth-notes of the canzona are obsessive. The represent
of the main key centers in this act is transparent. Belinda, Di
and the courtiers try to lift the queen from her severe C mind
parallel major. The opening arietta and chorus (No. 2), thou
tonic, are resolutely cheery and move easily into the softer me
mediant. Dido's air "Ah! Belinda" (No. 3) is a miniature *da c*
plete with an opening declamatory passage. The first couplet, "
am press'd / With torment not to be confess'd," is haltingly
rhythm ragged and fractured. The aria proper, "Peace and I
grown," begins at the tenth statement of the bass pattern with a n

Example 5   "Whence could so much virtue spring? " bars 1–12

in the closing lines of the recitative. Though the passage shown in Example 6 is as chromatic as any thus far, the ascending semitones signal rising passion, and the modulation to the parallel major is now firmly secured. These two pages of music cover much emotional ground, and the dizzying speed of the drama has troubled some authorities, particularly Westrup.[35] But in this scene, the balletic duet and chorus that follow, "Fear no danger to ensue" (No. 7) (frequently cited as the most Frenchified numbers in the opera), give the audience ample time to absorb Dido's change of heart.[36]

    35. See below, p. 202.
    36. Both Ian Spink, in *English Song Dowland to Purcell* (London: Batsford, 1973), p. 223, and Moore, in *Henry Purcell & the Restoration Theatre*, p. 51, mention the French flavor.

Example 6   "Whence could so much virtue spring? " bars 19-25

Aeneas's entrance (at No. 8) is an anticlimax, his recitative lacking a distinctive character. But the exchange with Dido is important to the greater musical structure. His question to the queen ("When . . . shall I be bless'd?") is in a bold G major; her response ("Fate forbids what you pursue") and his protest ("Aeneas has no fate but you") send the music coldly through A minor to E minor, an association of key and affect that is reaffirmed in Act II when the elf disguised as Mercury appears to Aeneas to remind him of his destiny. The modulation to E minor, though handled smoothly, disrupts the monolithic tonal scheme, heralding the intrusion of desire, which makes a symbolic appearance in the following contrapuntal chorus, "Cupid only throws the dart" (No. 9); appropriately, this piece contains a high concentration of pungent dissonances, especially at the words "dart" and "wounds." Hitherto, the chorus has simply echoed business already concluded by Belinda and the "second woman," but here the courtiers do far more than comment on the action; they represent an abstract force.

Although Dido utters not another word in this act after the frosty "Fate forbids what you pursue," jubilation prevails in Belinda's air "Pursue thy conquest" (No. 11), the chorus "To the hills and the vales" (No. 12), and the Triumphing Dance (No. 13). The queen's silence results not merely from the compressed dimensions of Tate's libretto but from her shame at having buried her grief so quickly. Yet the courtiers' exaltation is genuine if not entirely unrestrained. The most beguiling moment of the first-act finale is the passage shown in Example 7. Superficially, the cross-relation between B♭ in the soprano and B♮ in the tenor is only a touch of word-painting, but the intrusion of G minor, the key in which Dido will die, into a chorus celebrating her amorous triumph is a cruel irony.

Example 7   "To the hills and the vales," bars 5–8 (strings omitted)

To the   mu - si - cal__ groves   and the   cool sha - dy   foun-tains

The Triumphing Dance, which is built on a four-bar ground, is one of Purcell's happiest inspirations. The melodic periods are locked to the bass until the fourth variation, in which the violins double the length of the previous phrases. The majestic sweep of dotted rhythms is supported harmonically by transposing the bass to G major for one statement, clearly a case of the tail wagging the dog. Of the four grounds in the opera, only the one in Dido's Lament is immutable.

By positing the witches as symbols of religious zeal, I have tried to acquit them of the charge that they do not behave like humans. But what is most unsettling about the first scene of the second act is the juxtaposition of the Sorceress's impressively somber recitative and the freakish glee of her enchantresses' choruses. That the scene is a black parody of the first act is surely the best explanation for its more bizarre effects.[37] The two episodes have the same dramatic design, but with twisted ironies. The Sorceress, like Dido, is also consumed — not with grief, but with hate, which she expresses by plotting to destroy the queen. The tonal plan, which is much less rigid than that of Act I, reflects the parallel resolutions of inner conflict. The chorus, singing in the major mode, coaxes the Sorceress from her F-minor recitative, whose accompanying strings are like bitter treacle. But she returns gravely to the minor in order to reaffirm the modulation to the parallel major, then overshoots to C major at the line "Depriv'd of fame, of life and love" (No. 16, bars 8–10). The ensuing chorus "Ho, ho, ho," which is in the new and unexpected key, is thus a taunting reminder of "Fear no danger," the first piece in Act I to be unequivocally in C major. The parodistic function of the witches' scene is at its clearest here, as the Sorceress, despite the efforts of her weird courtiers, controls the action and the highly representational tonal scheme, precisely as Dido did earlier.

Intertwined with the warped references to the first act are frequent hints of later action. The Sorceress's instructions to the elf who will personate

37. See below, pp. 263–67.

The Storm as depicted
in Dryden's translation
of the *Aeneid* (1697):

> . . . *the gath'ring Clouds*
> *obscure the Skies;*
> *From Pole to Pole the forky*
> *Lightning flies.*

(Courtesy of the British
Library)

Mercury are fraught with anticipation. In Example 8, mention of Aeneas's
destiny draws the music to G minor, and the word "fate" is underscored by a
diminished-seventh chord—rare in the opera—over a tonic pedal. The distant sounds of the hunt, represented by the violins flourishing a D-major
chord, will be transformed into the tempest in the following scene. The
witches' ceremony ends with the chorus-and-dance formula of the first act.

Example 8   "Ruin'd ere the set of sun?" bars 4–7

Example 9   "In our deep vaulted cell," bars 15-19 (strings omitted)

"In our deep vaulted cell" (No. 21), justly famous for its echoes, was probably inspired by Matthew Locke's far more elaborate but less successful "Great Psyche shall find no such pleasure" in Act I of the semi-opera *Psyche* (1675). Each of Purcell's echoes is either three or six beats long, with a stress on the second or fifth beat; the shift of accent to the third beat at the hemiola cadence shown in Example 9 coincides felicitously with eerie cross-relations. The Echo Dance of Furies (No. 22) is a further grotesquerie.[38] The piece can easily sound over-elaborate, especially in a labored performance. One should recall that the 1689 libretto specifies a dance of *"Inchanteresses and Fairees;"* the "furies" seem to have originated with the 1700 production of *Measure for Measure*.

The swift pace of the action is all but arrested in the next scene, the leafy grove. Dido's courtiers entertain Aeneas after the hunt, which is also a poetic euphemism for their love-making. The song on a ground, "Oft she visits this lone mountain" (No. 25), performed by the "second woman," recounts the story of Actaeon, who was killed by his own hounds. It thus joins the hunting metaphor to the idea of Dido's being destroyed from within by shame. The air is like the queen's ground in Act I in that the plastic vocal phrases seldom coincide with the bass periods. As noted in the discussions of "Ah! Belinda" and the Triumphing Dance, Purcell's approach to ostinatos was never pedantic; he frequently extends or transposes them to other keys for contrast or to support melodic fancies that exceed the harmonic limits of the given bass. In "Oft she visits" the ground strays briefly at one point (shown in Example 10) for what would appear to be textual rather than purely musical reasons. The modulation to A major, no more than a harmonic legerdemain, is meant to draw attention to "mortal wounds." The ground is also broken once in the attached dance, with an equally brief excursion to F major.

The hypnotic pieces in D minor make the outburst of the storm in D

---

38. Dent's analysis is reprinted below, pp. 217-18.

Example 10 "Oft she visits this lone mountain," bars 17-25

And af - ter, af - ter mor - tal wounds, And af - ter, af -

- ter mor - tal wounds Dis-cov - - - er'd too, too

late; And af ter af - ter mor - tal wounds

major all the more electrifying, as Dido reacts excitedly to the atmospheric fireworks depicted by the shimmering chord in the strings. Belinda starts the stampede back to Carthage with "Haste, haste, to town" (No. 27). But Aeneas, whose recent travels have apparently inured him to foul weather, remains to hear the enunciation from *The Spirit of the Sorceress . . . in likeness of* Mercury." Her recitative, "Stay, Prince, and hear" (No. 28), is unremarkable, conveying none of the enchantresses' sinister motivation in either words or music. Aeneas's response is another matter. Unquestioningly, almost enthusiastically, he accepts the command to set sail, then recalls his promise to the queen: "Let Dido Smile and I'll defy / The feeble stroke of Destiny." With a two-and-a-half-bar aspirated melisma on the repeated words "But Ah," Purcell transforms Tate's cardboard Trojan into Virgil's procrastinating ingrate, a hero among belligerent men but a coward to a spurned woman. The music is suspended on the dominant, E major—unresolved until the final cadence and painfully decorated by adjacent semitones—while Aeneas wails an elaborate exclamation that Dido will recall with utter humility during the Lament. One may feel some momentary sympathy for Aeneas, but his agony is pur-

posely exaggerated. It is easy to over-estimate the significance of the recitative, especially if one accepts its exposed position at the end of Act II in the
Tenbury manuscript as a feature of Purcell's original design, ignoring the fact
that in both the 1689 and 1700 librettos the scene ends with the reappearance
of the witches. The irony of Aeneas's instant decision to leave Dido, which he
regrets only after the fact, is spoiled without an immediate reminder of the
Sorceress's role. The act originally ended with the Groves Dance, performed
for the witches "By the Nymphs of Carthage"; Dido's courtiers now unknowingly entertain a new queen.

The jaunty scene for the sailors at the beginning of Act III has an underlying vein of cynicism. After the first couplet, "Come away, fellow sailors . . . ,"
the soloist sings

> Take a boozy short leave of your nymphs on the shore,
> And silence their mourning
> With vows of returning,
> But never intending to visit them more.

This is a crude dockside version of Aeneas's heroic crocodile tears to be shed
later during the confrontation with Dido. In both air and chorus, the inner
couplet is set to a chromatically descending tetrachord (see Example 11).
Though beginning on the note C, it nevertheless leads to a strong cadence in
G minor (bar 56), a distinctly unsubtle foreshadowing of the ground in Dido's
Lament. The sailors' insensitivity to the prince's dilemma is almost an act of
disloyalty. Have they missed the irony, or have they become the puppets of the
Sorceress, like the courtiers at the end of the preceding act? In the 1689
libretto "Come away, fellow sailors" has the speech prefix "*Cho*," which Purcell divided into air and chorus. Tate's stage direction is important: "*Scene
the Ships*. Enter *the Saylors. The Sorceress and her Inchanteress*"; this implies
that the witches are to observe the entertainment from the side of the stage. In
the *Measure for Measure* play-book "Come away, fellow sailors" is assigned to
the Sorceress, a considerable license in light of the lyric's salty character. In
the Tenbury score the air is given to a treble sailor, and the manuscript even

Example 11   "Come away, fellow sailors," bars 48–51

delays the entrance of the witches until after the ensuing dance. A single-page engraving of "The Saylors Song" published about 1700 states, however, that the air was sung by the tenor Mr. Wiltshire. One interpretation of this conflicting evidence is that Purcell intended "Come away, fellow sailors" for the disguised Sorceress as a pied-piper enticement to the men to board the ships, but the 1700 adapter, aware of the need for another male soloist, reassigned the song to a tenor. This possibility casts doubt on the usual portrayal of the Sorceress by a singer with a dark mezzo-soprano or contralto voice, often tinged with a sinister nasality. Most women who undertake the role try to maintain the menacing aura of the opening recitative of Act II in all the subsequent solos. But the Sorceress, like Mother Demdike in *The Lancashire Witches* and Ragusa in *Brutus of Alba*, is a freakish hag capable of assuming any shape or persona in an instant. Apparently overlooked by modern music directors in their casting decisions is the fact that her vocal range is the same as Dido's—an octave and a fifth from middle C to high G. And her tessitura, like the queen's, begins rather low and gradually ascends. The Sorceress's final song, "Our next motion" (No. 32), a sprightly piece indeed, lies quite high, and has therefore caused many a hapless contralto, especially those who favor the nasal approach, some discomfort.

Further evidence of the Sorceress's possible role in hastening the sailors on their way is the witches' exit music, a skittish dance tantalizingly described in the 1689 libretto: "Jack *of the* Lanthorn *leads the* Spaniards *out of their way among the Inchanteresses.*"[39] This obviously reflects the exotic choreography devised by Priest, for whose pupils the opera was written. Some authorities have assumed that "Spaniards" is a synonym for "sailors";[40] the sense of the stage direction may be, therefore, that Will-o'-the-wisp leads the sailors out from among the witches, who are perhaps disguised as the "Nymphs of the Shore." Of course, so-called Spanish dances had enjoyed a vogue in the public theatres during the sixties and seventies, an inheritance from the Stuart masque, but the fad had all but passed by 1690. A precedent for the incongruous appearance of an Iberian in a school masque was set by Duffett and Banister's *Beauties Triumph* performed in Chelsea in 1676, in which a "Spaniard" sang and danced a sarabande in honor of Juno. But Purcell's dance is as unlike a sarabande as possible, the abrupt changes of meter and character obviously tailored to the grotesque movements of the dancers. The inclusion of Jack-o'-lantern is equally whimsical. Probably referring more to a

---

39. In the 1700 quarto this is simply called "A Dance of Wizards and Witches."
40. See, for example, Moore, *Henry Purcell & the Restoration Theatre*, p. 57, and below, p. 167.

special effect than to Will-o'-the-wisp, it may have been inspired by the machine effects at the end of the first act of *The Lancashire Witches*. Clod, like Diogenes, is groping his way through a storm, when "One of the Witches flies away with [his] Candel and Lanthorn, Mother *Demdike* sets him upon the top of a Tree, and they all fly away Laughing."

The third act is the emotional inverse of the first. After the B♭-major bustling of the sailors' and witches' somewhat disorganized celebration, the orderly G-minor threnody begins with Dido and Aeneas's bitter parting. The dialogue of this scene relies more heavily on *Brutus of Alba* than does any other in the opera, as the following excerpts show:

Brutus. Hold, hold! by all that's good . . .

. . .

Brutus. 'Twere Woman's Fraud t'have ruin'd with your Smiles, But to betray with Tears, the Crocodile's.

Aeneas. By all that's good, *Dido*. By all that's good, no more . . .

. . .

Dido. Thus on the fatal banks of Nile, weeps the deceitful crocodile.

Tate chose to model the principal confrontation of the opera not on Brutus's final leave-taking but on the episode in Act IV in which the queen wretchedly confesses her sin of "adultery" to the confidante Amarante. Thus the scene begins as if in mid-conversation, and a listener unfamiliar with the earlier play would assume that Belinda has just reassured the queen that the prince still loves her. But Tate's Dido, like Virgil's, already knows why Aeneas has come; it is an intuition born of guilt. She sings "Earth and Heav'n conspire my fall"; though fondly believing that Aeneas will "offend the gods, and Love

Example 12   "Your counsel all is urg'd in vain," bars 18–23

obey," she realizes that her undoing is of baser origins. His timorous announcement of departure is set to a rising chromatic line that creeps from C
minor to G minor, a cowardly retrograde of Dido's noble descent in the recitative preceding the Lament (Example 12). In the queen's scornful reply to his
decision, Purcell reduces the lofty dialogue to its human essentials. Dido's first
reaction to Aeneas's "By all that's good" is a derisive parroting of his pompous
indignation, but the next repetition (shown in Example 13), with the cross-

Example 13   "Your counsel all is urg'd in vain," bars 29–34

relation between B♭ in the voice in bar 30 and B♮ in the bass in bar 31, is stab-
bingly cynical. After this stunning moment, the dialogue resumes a stiff for-
mality. In the closing duet Aeneas hollowly assures Dido that he will stay, an
echo of the deceitful vows the sailors made to their shore nymphs at the beginning of the act. Though the former lovers sing resolutely and at the same
time, they no longer sing together.

Separating the bitter farewell and Dido's Lament is the chorus "Great
minds against themselves conspire" (No. 36), which, despite its brevity, gives
a feeling of the passage of considerable time.[41] It bridges the gulf between
emotional extremes and is structurally reflective, beginning in B♭ major and
ending in G minor, thereby restating in an orderly, formal manner the abrupt
shift of tonal center that occurred earlier between the Witches' Dance and
Dido's recitative "Your counsel all is urg'd in vain." Thus, as in the first two
acts, an important modulation is in effect accomplished twice. The second

41. See Kerman, below, p. 225.

Example 14   "Great minds against themselves conspire," bars 7–10 (strings omitted)

half of the chorus stresses a poignant melodic figure shown in Example 14: the diminished fourth flanked by adjacent semitones, a motif that in various rhythmic guises permeates the opera, appearing prominently in more than a dozen numbers. Of course it helps to unify the work, but one must recognize it as a regular feature of Purcell's grammar for music in minor keys; in the theatre works it is commonly associated with grief or weeping. It appears in two more elaborate variants in *Dido and Aeneas*: with ascending semitones and descending diminished fourth (see Example 15A), and the rarer version with falling semitones and rising diminished fourth (see Example 15B). As if

Example 15A   Overture, bars 5–6

Example 15B   "Shake the cloud," bars 4–5

your brow, Fate your

"Shake the cloud," bars 26–7

Grief___ should ne'er,

"Ah! Belinda," bars 3–5

Ah!___   Ah!   Be - lin - da,

"The Queen of Carthage," bars 6–8

most   wretch - ed prove,

The Witches' Dance, bars 19–21

to underscore the immense concentration of emotion in "Great minds" and to prepare for the torrent of descending chromatics in the Lament, only in the chorus do both forms of the grief motif appear together.

The Lament is Tate's farthest departure from the fourth book of the *Aeneid*, since the operatic Dido, probably in acknowledgment of the allegorical resemblance to Queen Mary, dies in a manner as unlike Virgil's queen as could be imagined. Instead of cursing her former lover, "Exoriare aliquis ex nostris ossibus altor" (May there arise from our bones some avenger), she leaves the pathetic injunction "Remember me, but ah! forget my fate." In fact, the only hint of Virgil's Dido is found in the line just before the Lament, "Death is now a welcome guest"; the word "guest" is important, as it recalls the queen's plea in IV. 323–4:

> Oh, I am dying! To what, my guest, are you leaving me!
> "Guest"—that is all I may call you now, who have called you husband.[42]

The recitative before the Lament (No. 37), far from simply foreshadowing once more the inexorable descent to the grave, seems to summarize the entire drama. Dido turns again to her confidante and to C minor ("Thy hand, Belinda"), descends into the Sorceress's black key of F minor ("darkness shades me"), and then, before retreating to G minor for the last time, grasps for her C-major glory only to have it slip away ("More I would, but Death invades me"). Westrup has ably described the paradox of "When I am laid in earth": though casting the climactic air in the utterly conventional mould of the Italian operatic lament, "Purcell rises within narrow limits to monumental grandeur."[43] The Lament also derives much splendor from its sheer inevitability. Throughout the opera, most of Dido's music sags under the weight of descending chromatics; her first air, also sung to a repeating bass, modulates to G minor. The grounds themselves are a deceptively naive symbol for earth and the grave. The accompanying strings, which could have easily produced a maudlin effect, are an ironic reminder of the Sorceress's recitatives. The violins gradually rise to enfold the voice with weeping appoggiaturas, thereby overriding the unpleasant association with the witches and supplying the pathos Dido's melody assiduously avoids. As several writers have noted, the setting of "ah!" (shown in Example 16) is astonishingly beautiful. Each of the previous melodic phrases has marked the arrival at the note D in the third bar of the ground with a dominant chord. Dido's simple, non-dominant decoration of the fifth scale degree recalls Aeneas's labored and artificial exclamation in his second-act recitative: "But ah! what language can I try." Here, however, as appoggiaturas collide in the violins, the voice slides away into

42. *The Aeneid of Virgil*, trans. C. Day Lewis (London: Hogarth, 1952), p. 81.
43. See below, p. 202.

Example 16   "When I am laid in earth," bars 35–8

oblivion, releasing Dido from the chromatic chain that pulled her relentlessly to the Lament.

Purcell faced a dilemma from which only a handful of composers of musical tragedy have been able to escape: how to write a denouement that neither disturbs the delicate balance between pathos and irony with unnecessary moralizing nor simply spins out the climactic masterpiece for sustained and therefore diminished effect. The final chorus, "With drooping wings" (No. 39), avoids both traps and is therefore perhaps an even greater achievement than the Lament, as it transports the drama to another plane. The chorus echoes the pervasive descent of Dido's air, but the chromatics have abated. About mid-way through, in the passage given as Example 17, the

Example 17   "With drooping wings," bars 14–17 (strings omitted)

Example 18   "With drooping wings," bars 26-30 (strings omitted)

second, less common form of the grief motif returns. The emotional crest is reached with the heart-stopping rests shown in Example 18. There in the alto part is the last statement of the familiar motif, now magically softened with an F♮ (bar 27) which a composer of more pedantic mind might well have left sharp for consistency's sake. With a single stroke, Purcell removes the sting of death.

Here the Tenbury manuscript ends, but the final item in the 1689 libretto is a *"Cupids Dance,"* in keeping with the sequence of air, chorus, and dance that closes the previous scenes. "With drooping wings" seems an inappropriate accompaniment for dancers, unlike "Fear no danger" in Act I, which is followed by the stage direction *"Dance this Cho. The Baske."* Tate's libretto requires three other dances not found in the Tenbury score: in Act I, a *"Gittars Chacony,"* and in Act II, a *pas de deux* for *"Drunken Saylors"* as well as another *"Gittar Ground."* None of these stage directions is found in the 1700 quarto of *Measure for Measure,* nor does that text mention the Cupids' Dance. But the Tenbury manuscript provides a tiny clue that the opera may have originally ended with a dance. "With drooping wings" lacks a final double bar-line; all parts finish as does the first violin shown in Example 19. In manuscripts of the period, the ends of pieces or large sections thereof are nearly always marked with a terminal flourish, an embroidered double or treble bar-line finished off with several tight turns.[44] Such a device is found in

44. That the chorus has a first and second ending would not appear to account for the anomaly, because even the second ending of the canzona in the overture is closed with a single bar-line.

Example 19   "With drooping wings," bars 29-30, first violin

the Tenbury score at the end of Act II, scene i. Working on the assumption that the scribe attempted to make a diplomatic transcription of his source, one might conclude that the final folio or two — that is, the Cupids' Dance — had already been removed; the copyist therefore attempted to signal the incomplete state of the final act by leaving the chorus without a terminal flourish or even a closing bar-line.[45]

How does Dido die? The final ambiguity would seem to matter little in light of the tragic power of the music. Tate's decision to replace Virgil's bitter and violent end to Book IV with pathetic resignation would rule out a spectacular suicide with Aeneas's sword, though earlier in the third act the Sorceress prophesies that Dido "bleeds to Night, and *Carthage* Flames tomorrow." Yet none of the main sources of the opera — the 1689 libretto, the 1700 playbook, or the Tenbury manuscript — includes a stage direction for her death. In *Brutus of Alba*, the Queen of Syracuse succumbs after a fit of insanity, recovering just long enough to realize that "My malady at last has prov'd my Cure, / My Griefs at last have swell'd to that degree / To break my o're-charged Heart and give no Ease." The final scene of the play is set in *"the Cell,"* presumably the dead king's tomb discovered first in Act II. This evokes the disturbing image of the queen dying on Sychaeus's catafalque in Rubens's *Death of Dido*. A burial vault also figures prominently in the opera. As Dido begins her final recitative, *"Cupids* appear in the Clouds o're her Tomb." The 1700 libretto does not include this important stage direction and also omits a line from the penultimate couplet. The final chorus is given thus:

> With drooping Wings you Cupids come,
> Soft and Gentle as her Heart,
> Keep here our Watch and never part.

"To scatter Roses on her Tomb" is deleted, implying that bars 11-14 were cut, thereby leaving the music two beats out but preserving the overall harmonic sense. Gildon's removal of the funereal trappings could lead to a startling conclusion: that Dido does not die. Absurd as this may seem, the absence of any reference to the tomb reinforces the allegorical links to the main plot of

---

45. The word "Finis" is written at the bottom of the last chorus, but in a much larger, perhaps different, hand.

Rubens' *Death of Dido* (Musée de Louvre)

Measure for Measure, since Dido represents Isabella, who survives Angelo's lustful advances with her chastity intact.

If *Dido and Aeneas* was intended as a cautionary tale to remind King William of his responsibilities to his wife and his new kingdom, then the death of Queen Mary's counterpart at the end of the theatrical paean would have been the epitome of bad taste, even if portrayed by a schoolgirl "unscarr'd by turning times" and isolated from the cynicism of court and theatre. If, on the other hand, the operatic queen were left to linger on the point of death during her lover's "absence," the parallel would have been slightly less embarrassing. But as the nineties wore on and the king's absences from England became more frequent and protracted, a public performance of *Dido and Aeneas* would have become increasingly awkward politically, and after Mary's death in December 1694 it would have been unthinkable, since the tragic ending would have implied that William's neglect was in some way responsible for his wife's passing. So the composer and librettist must bear some of the blame for the initial obscurity that greeted this masterpiece.

Yet remove the fatal catastrophe and *Dido* collapses into a harmless masque. While cold and rational history tells us that unadulterated, apotheosis-less tragic opera was unknown to seventeenth-century England, we cannot ignore our response to Purcell's miniature. Purcell approached the drama forthrightly with a thorough understanding of Book IV of the *Aeneid*. Despite the laundered and starched libretto, the music restores Dido's obsessions, neuroses, even the sexual desire that Tate prudishly removed or clumsily transformed into heroic virtue. And most important of all, she dies through the music.

A. MARGARET LAURIE

~~~~~~~~

Allegory, Sources, and Early Performance History

A research student of the late Thurston Dart at Cambridge, A. Margaret Laurie later edited several volumes of the theater music for *The Works of Henry Purcell*, including the score reprinted in this volume. The following essay is based on the *Dido and Aeneas* chapter in her doctoral dissertation, "Purcell's Stage Works" (Cambridge, 1962), the first comprehensive study of this repertory.

The libretto of *Dido and Aeneas* contains the text not only of the opera proper, but also of an allegorical prologue in two scenes designed to be sung throughout, with choruses, dances and quite elaborate singing. This prologue, which has been the subject of much debate, needs to be considered in relation to continental operatic traditions. Spectacularly staged, all-sung opera was originally developed in Italy at the turn of the seventeenth century as a court entertainment for festive occasions. The celebratory associations of opera diminished in Italy after the establishment of public opera houses from 1637 onwards. In France, however, although the first Italian operas performed at court in the late 1640s were not particularly well received, the young Louis XIV and his advisers were quick to realize the possibilities of using elaborately staged musical entertainments for political ends, expanding the congratulatory tone customary for specific celebrations into a more general glorification of the monarch. The *ballets de cour* of the 1650s and *comédie ballets* of the 1660s culminated in a specifically French type of opera, making much use of dance, which was introduced by an allegorical prologue extolling the king and often referring to recent political events. All the operas which Lully produced annually from 1673 until his death in 1687 include such a prologue.

In England in the first half of the seventeenth century, the court masque was also basically celebratory and similarly included an element of glorification of the monarchy. Dance and song were important features, though masques were rarely, if ever, set entirely to music. The form disappeared with the Commonwealth, though less elaborate masques continued to be produced privately. During the late 1650s Sir William Davenant staged several musical entertainments, including one, *The Siege of Rhodes*, which was set to music throughout, though unfortunately none of its music has survived. The main purpose of this work, however, seems to have been to circumvent the Commonwealth ban on stage plays, for when this was lifted after the Restoration in 1660 and Davenant became manager of the Duke's Company—one of the two theatrical companies established under royal license at the beginning of the reign of Charles II—he made no further attempt to mount any more such productions. Nonetheless, music did feature prominently in several Duke's Company plays, and in the 1670s Davenant's successors developed a form of dramatic opera which incorporated extensive musical scenes and eye-catching stage effects. Even in these, however, the main action was carried out in speech, for the conventions governing the use of music in English drama, and the shortage of singing actors, did not encourage the development of all-sung opera.

Early in 1674 a French opera, *Ariane*, with a new allegorical prologue celebrating the fairly recent marriage of the Duke of York (later James II) to his second wife, Mary of Modena, was produced first at court and then in the rival King's Theatre. This was sung in French by French singers, but an English translation was published for the use of the audience. This states that the music was by Louis Grabu, but the main opera had been set by Robert Cambert some years earlier, and it is possible that Grabu only provided the new prologue.

About ten years later Dryden, probably with a view to the twenty-fifth anniversary of the Restoration, wrote the text of a patriotic dramatic opera, *King Arthur*, with a French-style, all-sung, panegyric prologue representing the Restoration in allegory. For some unexplained reason, however, he then laid aside *King Arthur* and expanded the prologue into a full-length, all-sung opera called *Albion and Albanius* by adding two further acts depicting more recent royal events. This was set by Grabu. It was in rehearsal by January 1685[1] but Charles II died suddenly on 6 February before it could be publicly performed. It was finally produced in June with some emendations reflecting the changed political situation, but its initial run coincided with the disastrous attempt by Charles's illegitimate son, the Duke of Monmouth, to seize the throne. The opera's failure caused the theatre considerable financial loss. Nothing so elaborate was attempted again until the series of dramatic operas with Purcell's music were produced, beginning in 1690, that is, a year after

---

1. *Rutland MSS*, Historical Manuscripts Commission, 12th Report, Appendix V (London: H.M.S.O., 1889), p. 85.

the premiere of *Dido and Aeneas*. Quite probably it was this production that convinced the theatre management that Purcell was a composer of sufficient stature to make a success of dramatic opera and so justify the considerable financial risk of mounting it. Although the performance of *Dido* had been an amateur one, the proprietor of the school at which it was staged, Josias Priest, was a professional dancer with close associations with the public theatre. He had been involved in the choreography for the operatic *Macbeth* in 1672[2] and was to be responsible for that of at least the first three of Purcell's dramatic operas.[3] He must therefore have been well known to Betterton, the principal actor and theatrical producer at this period. Betterton would have known about *Dido* and may well have been invited to see it.

The only two masques performed at court during this period also had sung prologues. The first, Crowne's *Calisto* (1674) — really a play with musical interludes — was written at the request of Princess Mary, though not for any particular occasion. Its prologue is a complimentary allegory ending with direct homage to the King and Queen. The other, Blow's *Venus and Adonis*, an all-sung work in three acts and a prologue, is much more important, for it clearly served as a model for *Dido and Aeneas*. It is entitled "A Masque for ye Entertainment of the King" in its earliest source[4] but is not mentioned at all in the royal records, in contrast to the profusely documented *Calisto*. This suggests that *Venus and Adonis* was an unofficial production; even so, Blow's colleagues in the King's Musick, including Purcell himself, may well have played in the orchestra. Two of the three main characters, Venus and Cupid, were sung respectively by Charles II's ex-mistress, Mary Davies, and their daughter, Lady Mary Tudor, and the work was probably performed in 1682 or 1683 when Lady Mary would have been about nine years old. It could have been an attempt by Mrs. Davies to regain Charles's favor or at least to remind him of his responsibilities to his daughter. It is perhaps relevant that from September 1683 until shortly after Lady Mary's marriage in 1687 an annuity of £1500 was paid from the Secret Service Funds to the Countess of Marischal for Lady Mary's upkeep.[5] Despite its sub-title ("A Masque . . ."), *Venus and Adonis* is a true opera with a genuine, if slight, plot which most exceptionally ends tragically. The prologue is unusual in that its chief character, Cupid, is also one of the protagonists of the main opera. Moreover, it is not laudatory,

2. See John Downes, *Roscius Anglicanus*, 1708, ed. Montague Summers (London: Fortune Press, [1928]), p. 33.

3. Downes, p. 42.

4. British Library, Add. MS 22100.

5. [Henry Guy], *Moneys received and paid for Secret Services of Charles II and James II . . . 1679 to . . . 1688*, ed. John Y. Akerman, Camden Society Vol. LII (London, 1851), *passim*.

but rather satirizes the infidelity prevalent in court circles. This could well have been designed to rouse Charles's conscience; if so, this prologue also expresses, in symbolical terms, the underlying purpose of the whole work. Thus, the all-sung allegorical prologues produced in England before *Dido and Aeneas* seem mainly to have had the same eulogistic intention as their French counterparts, with *Venus and Adonis* possibly trading on this conception to make its own radically different point.

The prologue to *Dido and Aeneas* could also have been designed to honor the monarchy; indeed it may represent royal events leading up to a specific occasion for celebration. This would appear to be the most reasonable explanation for its extreme elaboration and apparent irrelevance to the main text. Although James II, a Roman Catholic, had succeeded to the throne in February 1685 without much overt opposition, his determination to encourage his religion and to place Catholics in positions of power had increasingly alienated his Protestant subjects. The birth of a son on 10 June 1688 to his second wife seemed to secure the Catholic succession, and this event finally induced senior politicians to invite William of Orange to take over the country, since William, as James's nephew and husband of his elder daughter, Mary, was the nearest Protestant male heir. Mary joined William in London on 12 February 1689 and they were offered the crown as joint rulers on the following day.

John Buttrey has pointed out that the first scene of the prologue to *Dido and Aeneas*, in which Phoebus and Venus come in turn over the sea in chariots, could represent the arrival in Britain from Holland of first William then Mary.[6] He then suggests that the second scene, in which Spring (after welcoming Venus) is acclaimed by various nymphs, shepherds and shepherdesses, refers to Queen Mary's birthday on 30 April and that the whole work was designed to celebrate this day in 1689. It seems to me, however, that a girls' school would much more probably have celebrated the joint coronation of William and Mary on 11 April. The stress placed in the text on the equality of the male and female deities being extolled would have been far more pertinent to this occasion than to one which concerned the Queen alone.

Whether the main opera was also intended to be allegorical is more questionable. Apart from their prologues, Lully's operas were not, as a rule, except in the very general sense of presenting the rewards of heroic action. Given the moral ambiguities of Virgil's story of Dido and Aeneas, even when smoothed over by Tate as much as possible, it seems a curiously inappropriate

---

6. See "Dating Purcell's Dido and Aeneas," *Proceedings of the Royal Musical Association*, 94 (1967–68), 61. Part of this essay is reprinted in the present volume, pp. 228–35.

theme to have chosen for the occasion. Such inappropriateness, however, was not unprecedented. The story of the deserted wife Ariane was equally unsuitable for the Duke of York's marriage, though that opera at least ends with a splendid apotheosis in which Ariane is consoled by Bacchus. The possibility of an allegorical interpretation reflecting adversely on William,[7] whether intended or not, could have been one of the factors which militated against a public performance in the early 1690s when he was frequently abroad, and even more in 1695 immediately after Mary's death. More mundane considerations, such as the opera's being too short for a whole evening's entertainment or the reluctance of London audiences to accept all-sung opera, were probably also significant. However, the work was not entirely forgotten.

At the end of 1694 increasingly bitter disagreements between the owners (patentees) and the actors of the Theatre Royal caused Betterton and the principal actors to break away and set up a rival playhouse in Lincoln's Inn Fields. This opened on 30 April 1695, and competition between the two companies was very fierce thereafter. The patentees had better facilities, since they retained two theatres: one in Dorset Garden and the other in Drury Lane. Even the comparatively modestly equipped Drury Lane house was larger than the rebel establishment in Lincoln's Inn Fields. The actors remaining with the patentees, however, were mainly young and inexperienced, and at first they largely depended on Purcell's music to draw an audience. In the years immediately after Purcell's death in November 1695 they revived his dramatic operas and produced several new ones of similar pattern, such as *Brutus of Alba* (1696), *Cinthia and Endimion* (1696), *The World in the Moon* (1697) and *The Island Princess* (1699). Betterton's company had the advantage of better actors and, initially, public sympathy. He concentrated more on straight plays but felt it necessary to retaliate with musical productions of his own from time to time. The first of these was Ravenscroft's *The Anatomist* (1696), into which was slotted the masque of *The Loves of Mars and Venus* in three acts and a prologue. This was followed by others such as *The Italian Husband* with a masque *Ixion* (1697), *Love's a Lottery* with *Love and Riches Reconcil'd* (1699) and then Charles Gildon's adaptation of Shakespeare's *Measure for Measure* with *Dido and Aeneas* added. This adaptation was probably performed in March or April 1700.[8] We have already observed that

7. See above, pp. 6–7, and below, p. 235.

8. According to *A Comparison between the two Stages*, 1702, ed. Staring B. Wells (Princeton: Princeton University Press, 1942), pp. 26–7, *Measure for Measure* was performed shortly before Vanbrugh's adaptation of *The Pilgrim*, which included Dryden's *The Secular Masque*. The third night of the latter is traditionally held to have been the day of Dryden's death, 1 May 1700; see *The London Stage, 1660–1800*, Part I, *1660–1700*, ed. W. Van Lennep (Carbondale: Southern Illinois University Press, 1965), p. 527.

Betterton almost certainly knew about the Chelsea performance of *Dido*. It may well have been his idea to revive the opera as part of *Measure for Measure*. Certainly it was the only major work of Purcell's not in the possession of the other theatre, and it must have been still virtually unknown. Gildon appears to have used *The Anatomist* as his model. *Dido* is treated as a series of four separate masques: Act I, Act II (consisting of the Cave Scene and the Grove Scene, as in the original libretto), Act III, and finally the prologue which, being the only really festive section, was the one best suited for the customary celebratory finale.

Following its professional debut in 1700, *Dido* was performed again on at least two occasions in 1704—as an afterpiece to *The Anatomist* on 29 January and with *The Man of Mode* on 8 April.[9] A revival of *Measure for Measure* "To which will be added, The Masque of Acis and Galatea" was advertised in the *Daily Courant* for 26 April 1706, with no mention of *Dido*.[10] Purcell's opera was, however, presumably retained in the body of the play, since *Acis and Galatea* has only one act. The latter could have been performed as an afterpiece (as *Dido* had been with *The Anatomist* and its masque in 1704), or it may have replaced the prologue as the last entertainment.

* * *

Very little of Purcell's music for *Dido and Aeneas* appears in contemporary sources. "Ah! Belinda" was the only aria from the opera to be included in *Orpheus Britannicus*[11] and even then with no mention of *Dido*. This song also appears in Durham Cathedral Library Mus. MS D.9, which dates from about 1705; both sources have interesting variants from the full score. "Fear no danger" was published, shorn of its second voice, as "a Song in the play call'd *Measure for Measure*" with two catches for three voices by Mr. Willis. "Come away, fellow sailors" was published as a single-sheet song entitled "The Saylors Song, set by Mr. Purcell, Sung by Mr. Wiltshire in the Play call'd Measure for Measure." Both presumably date from 1700. An instrumental version of "Fear no danger" derived from the chorus and the prelude to "Come away, fellow sailors" is given, anonymously and untitled, in part-books at Magdalene College, Cambridge.[12]

The earliest source of the whole work is St. Michael's College, Tenbury,

9. See Eric Walter White, "Early Theatrical Performances of Purcell's Operas," *Theatre Notebook*, 13 (1958-9), 55-6.

10. White, "Early Theatrical Performances," p. 63.

11. Vol. I (London: Henry Playford, 1698), 193.

12. MS F.4.35 (1-5), set V, no. 13, and set XXX, no. 2, respectively.

MS 1266 (5),[13] where it is entitled "The Loves of Aeneas and Dido." Watermarks show that the manuscript can date from no earlier than 1748, but it retains several archaic features such as the use of the mezzo-soprano clef for viola, cancelling sharps and flats for naturals, and early eighteenth-century forms of key and time signatures, all of which suggest that it was copied from a source dating from well before 1720. Philip Hayes (1738–97), a composer and Professor of Music at Oxford, also included "The Loves of Dido and Aeneas" in the third of a four-volume set of Purcell works which he copied in 1784–5.[14] These are now at Tatton Park, Knutsford, Cheshire. Hayes modernized the accidentals and key and time signatures and extended the bass figuring. Otherwise his score is very close to Tenbury 1266 (5), containing many, though not all, of the same obvious mistakes. Once or twice, however, where Tenbury has a blank bar, Hayes provides a reading which seems authentic. Most of the other divergencies concern slurring, though there are some differences of rhythm as well. The nature of these discrepancies suggests that Hayes was not working directly from the Tenbury score but rather from another closely related source. Although on the whole both scores are clearly written, they are not impeccable and occasionally it is difficult to know what Purcell intended. The use of slurs in the chorus string parts, for instance, seems arbitrary and is probably inauthentic in both scores. The Echo Dance of Furies presents particular problems; if, as seems likely, there are some mistakes in the text here, they must go back to the copy-text, for in only one of the suspect passages do the two scores differ.

Both scores contain stage directions, which suggests that they are copies of one used for a stage production. There are, however, vital differences between the scores on the one hand and the extant libretti on the other, the most significant being (a) the scores do not include the prologue; (b) at the end of the Grove Scene they omit not only the dialogue interpolated in 1700 but also the chorus and dance which end this scene in both libretti; (c) the Cave Scene is included in Act I, leaving the Grove Scene to form the whole of Act II; (d) there are sundry differences in the distribution of the text between the characters. Also, all the dances omitted in the 1700 libretto are absent from the scores.

We must therefore consider how far the Royal College libretto actually represents what Purcell wrote for the 1689 performance. Purcell quite frequently made minor changes in his texts, and some of the discrepancies must stem from him. The omission of the prologue and the end of Act II, however,

---

13. Now in the Bodleian Library, Oxford.
14. See Nigel Fortune, "A New Purcell Source," *Music Review*, 25 (1964), 109.

are major structural alterations which go far beyond his usual practice.

If, as postulated above, the prologue is an allegorical representation of the occasion for which the work was written, then it is inconceivable that it did not form part of Purcell's original setting. The fact that Gildon included it in his 1700 adaptation implies that it was integral to the available score, for it is unlikely that Betterton would have been prepared to have more than a quarter of the music newly composed.

Whether or not the witches' chorus and dance at the end of the Grove Scene were cut by Purcell is more problematical, for he did occasionally omit small pieces of text. Their inclusion in the 1700 libretto, however, again suggests that they *were* part of the original conception, and an examination of Purcell's structural practices supports the contention that he did provide at least a chorus at this point; certainly, all his other operatic scenes end with a chorus, often accompanied or followed by a dance. As already discussed by Curtis Price in the preceding essay, the key structure — always a carefully controlled feature of Purcell's works — confirms this, for this scene, like the earlier ones, seems to be constructed to move from minor to major on the same tonic. A section in D major would therefore appear to be necessary to complete the key change initiated by the recitative "The skies are clouded," and it seems logical to suppose that the text used was that provided in the libretto.

The scores place the Cave Scene in Act I, dividing the work roughly in half instead of into three more or less equal acts as in the libretti. Indeed, in the Tenbury (though not in the Tatton Park) score, the end of the Cave Scene is called "The End of the First Part." A theory has recently been advanced that Purcell himself was responsible for this rearrangement on the grounds that the two halves thus created are roughly symmetrical.[15] This is partly true, though it involves dividing the seamless first act in two at the change of key and equating dissimilar movements such as solos with duets, the overture with the short ritornello (No. 23)[16] and the recitatives "Whence could so much virtue spring" (No. 6) and "Stay, Prince, and hear" (No. 28). But the structural relationship between Nos. 6 and 7 on the one hand and Nos. 28 and 29 on the other is so totally different that these two recitatives cannot be reasonably compared. No. 6 moves without a break into No. 7, in the tonic major, whereas No. 28, in A minor, ends Act II (according to this hypothesis) and is followed after a pause by the instrumental prelude to No. 29, in the unrelated key of B♭ major. Since function is at least as important as form, I believe that

---

15. Ellen T. Harris, *Handel and the Pastoral Tradition* (London: Oxford University Press, 1980), pp. 134ff. Excerpts from this book are reprinted below, pp. 243-52.

16. This and the numbers cited below refer to rehearsal numbers in the present score.

this superficial symmetry is not particularly significant, and that Purcell followed the libretto's division of the work, grouping the two shorter Cave and Grove scenes in Act II. This certainly makes better dramatic sense, because these scenes are contiguous in time — in the Grove Scene the courtiers are resting from the hunt which they were pursuing during the Cave Scene — while there is a temporal gap between these scenes and those on either side of them. Purcell's key structure seems designed to underline this, for the two scenes are closely connected tonally, the first ending in F major, the second beginning in its relative minor, while the progressions over the other two intermissions are more distant: C major - F minor and D major(?) - B♭ major, respectively. A possible further link between the two scenes is the use of the comparatively remote D-major chord in the predominantly F-major Cave Scene to refer to the hunt, which could be a deliberate anticipation of the "storm" key of the following scene. Certainly the pictorial use of the strings in recitative in both scenes is somewhat similar. Gildon's grouping of these two scenes in his second entertainment in *Measure for Measure* again suggests that they belonged together in the score available for the adaptation.

Some of the verbal differences between the Royal College libretto and the scores are probably due to careless printing, but the music shows that Purcell did refine Tate's distribution of the text. The libretto specifies only one solo "Inchanteress" (or Witch — the change of designation found in both the *Measure for Measure* libretto and the scores was probably Purcell's own). The composer added a second solo witch and made these parts relatively more important by transferring some of the Sorceress's words to them. Thus both the recitatives "The Trojan Prince" (No. 18) and "See, see the flags" (No. 31) are divided between the Sorceress and one or both witches, though in the libretto they were assigned to the Sorceress alone, as were the words for the witches' duet "But ere we this perform" (No. 20).[17] Purcell makes the solo witches constantly echo one another; indeed "But ere we this perform" is quasi-canonical throughout. The chorus witches, by contrast, always sing homophonically, except when they break into imitative "ho, ho, ho's."

There are similar modifications in the courtly scenes as well. In the Grove "Haste, haste to town" (No. 27) is assigned to Dido in both libretti, with no mention of chorus, but to Belinda with choral repeat in the scores. Purcell presumably felt that a more extended movement was needed here than Tate had envisaged; having decided to introduce the chorus, the composer probably gave the solo to Belinda rather than to Dido, since Belinda acts as chorus leader elsewhere, although this left Dido with very little to sing in this scene.

---

17. In *Measure for Measure* this is assigned to the Sorceress and a witch.

The somewhat banal words are in any case more suited to Belinda. The treatment of the Second Woman is slightly more open to question. In the scores she is given only the lower part of the duet "Fear no danger" (No. 7) and the ground "Oft she visits" (No. 25). In the libretti two short sections of text in Act I, "The greatest blessing" and "What stubborn heart" (each of two lines of text), are marked "2 Women" in the Royal College libretto and "2 Woman" in *Measure for Measure*. The first could mean that Tate intended these passages to be set as duets, but this seems unlikely; these rubrics are probably misprints for "2nd Woman," as the later libretto implies. Certainly Purcell set them as solo passages; both are given to Belinda (who sings the previous bars) in the scores. The designation "Second Woman" could perhaps have been deleted from the scores here at some stage, but more probably Purcell reduced her part to a minimum to heighten the contrast between the respective attendants of Dido and the Sorceress without destroying the symmetry altogether.

These and other minor details apart, however, it would seem that the Royal College libretto does substantially represent what Purcell wrote in 1689 and that the scores do not. The scores certainly do not preserve the 1700 version. But they could, as Eric Walter White suggests,[18] relate to the next known performances in 1704. Since in these the opera followed other full-length plays, it probably had to be shortened. The number of different scenes required could also have caused problems, at least when it was performed with *The Anatomist* and *The Loves of Mars and Venus*. The prologue would have been the most obvious section to dispense with, for by then it must have seemed totally irrelevant; certainly its political connotations were no longer topical, since William was dead and England was again at war with France. The chorus and dance at the end of the Grove Scene, which are only tangential to the drama, could also have been cut simply to save time.

The division of the opera into two rather than three parts may also have arisen from the performances in 1700 and 1704. It was customary to mark the act divisions of a play by performing short instrumental tunes between the acts. *Albion and Albanius* and *Venus and Adonis*, not to mention all the Lully operas, have such act tunes; Purcell probably provided them for *Dido and Aeneas* as well. However, they would have been superfluous in the *Measure for Measure* production and could well have been lost at that stage. When the opera was reconstituted and played as an afterpiece in 1704, it was probably not performed straight through without any break at all, but its position at the end of the evening may have led to its being given only one

18. "New Light on 'Dido and Aeneas'," in *Henry Purcell, 1659–1695: Essays on his Music*, ed. Imogen Holst (London: Oxford University Press, 1959), p. 17.

interval instead of two; hence the change of the act divisions. The advertisement for the performance with *The Man of Mode* on 8 April 1704 notes that this would be performed with "the Masque of Aeneas and Dido, in several Musical Entertainments compos'd by the late Mr. Henry Purcell. And several Entertainments of new Scotch Dances."[19] Given the combined lengths of play and opera, even shorn of its prologue, the Scotch dances cannot have been allowed to occupy very much extra time. Perhaps they replaced at least some of the play's act tunes or were performed in the opera's intermissions. Even so they probably would not have been entered in the score, since act tunes were frequently omitted from the manuscripts of operatic works at this period. For instance, none of the *King Arthur* scores contain them, though we know of their existence from *Ayres for the Theatre*, published by Purcell's widow in 1697.

Some of the stage directions in the scores, notably that for the Echo Dance of Furies, suggest that they stem from a professional, post-1700 performance. In the Royal College libretto the rubric for this is simply "Eccho Dance. Inchanteresses and Fairees [presumably a misreading for Furies]." In *Measure for Measure* this becomes "Eccho Dance of Furies. At the End of the Dance Six Furies sinks [*sic*]. The four open the Cave fly up,"[20] providing a fascinating glimpse of how the dance was performed. This direction, with its implied use of trap-doors and flying equipment, is clearly reflected in the scores: "The Furies sink down in the Cave, the Rest fly up," to which has been added "Thunder & Lightning, horrid Musick." The inclusion of the words "The Loves of" in the titles of both scores may also point to a post-1700 origin, since *The Loves of Dido and Aeneas* is the title used in *Measure for Measure*, probably in imitation of *The Loves of Mars and Venus* in *The Anatomist*. In 1689 Durfey simply called the work *Dido and Aeneas*. The weight of evidence, therefore, suggests that the scores go back to a production no earlier than the third one.

In Lully's operas the overture was usually played both before and after the prologue, and Purcell could have adopted the same procedure in *Dido and Aeneas*. The all-sung prologue to Purcell's *The Indian Queen* is in fact framed by two statements of a trumpet tune in the prologue's key, preceded by the usual first and second music and overture in different keys. The trumpet tune, however, is used yet again as the first-act tune; the multiple use of such a tune is unusual in Purcell and may have resulted from the haste in

---

19. See White, "Early Theatrical Performances," p. 56.

20. The second half of this direction hardly makes sense as it stands; presumably either "open" is a misprint for "over" or it should read "The four open the cave and fly up."

which the work was written. If the C minor overture for *Dido* was first performed before the prologue, then the latter was probably cast mainly in C
minor and/or major. But this would have involved using the same keys as in
the first act, which, given the carefully varied key structure of the rest of the
work, seems unlikely. The avoidance of G major in a work orientated in C and
G minor, and particularly the use of B♭ major rather than G major in Act III
when all the other scenes revolve round a tonic - minor - to - major axis, could
mean that G major was the principal key of the prologue. This would have
suited its celebratory character and yet provided a link with the G minor in
which the work finishes. If the prologue were set in a key other than C, then
Purcell probably provided it with a different overture. Such a piece in G
minor entitled "Overture in Mr P Opera" and countersigned "Mr. H. Purcell"
in Royal College of Music MS 1172 was conjecturally assigned to *The Tempest*
in the Purcell Society Edition, purely on the grounds that this was the only
Purcell opera which lacked an overture. Most of the music for *The Tempest*
may well not be by Purcell, however;[21] if it is, then its style suggests that it
must have been written in the last year of his life. The harmonic idiom of the
overture, notably its frequent use of augmented chords, and other stylistic
features, such as the inversion of the fugue subject, are more characteristic of
works of an earlier stage of Purcell's career. The overture, therefore, probably
dates from the 1680s. It might belong to *Circe* (*c.* 1688?), since this work was
sometimes referred to as an opera, but equally it could have been written for
the prologue to *Dido and Aeneas*. It is certainly in a suitable key; indeed it
would complete the key cycle of the whole work.

   No details are known of the performers in the Chelsea production of
Dido and Aeneas, and virtually none for the professional performances. In
The Loves of Mars and Venus the prologue was performed by some of the
singers of the main masque.[22] The same was probably the case in *Dido*; indeed
the prologue and the opera proper employ exactly the same number of soloists, and Tate has arranged that characters in the prologue who might correspond to Dido, Belinda, the Second Woman and Aeneas leave the stage at the
end of the first scene so that they would have time to change costumes before
the first act of the main opera. This could also have compensated the singer of
Aeneas somewhat for his small part, since Phoebus is the dominant character
of the first scene of the prologue.

   21. See Margaret Laurie, "Did Purcell set *The Tempest* ?," *Proceedings of the Royal Musical Association*, 90 (1963-4), 43ff.
   22. The cast-list of the masque is given in the text published with Edward Ravenscroft's *The
Anatomist* (London: R. Baldwin, 1697).

The dancers and chorus sopranos were no doubt girls at Mr. Priest's school. The Sailor's part is written in the treble clef in the scores, so all the solo parts, except that of Aeneas, were probably sung by them also. The male singers, who would have included countertenors, and probably the orchestral players must have been imported for the occasion. It has been suggested that they may have come from the theatre or Westminster Abbey.[23] Alternatively, "young gentlemen" from a similar school could have been invited to take part, perhaps those from Louis Maidwell's school in Hatton Gardens for whom Purcell set an ode "Celestial music," performed on 5 August 1689, shortly after the premiere of the opera.[24] Maidwell had had a play performed at the Dorset Garden theatre in 1680 and could therefore have known Priest; he definitely knew Tate, since the latter had provided an introductory poem for *A Breviary of Roman History* translated into English by some of the Hatton Garden boys and published in 1684 by Maidwell himself.

Although the 1700 text of *Measure for Measure* gives the cast-list for the play, it does not include that for the musical entertainments. We have seen that the Sailor was sung by Mr. Wiltshire. Aeneas's part is written in the tenor clef but its highest note is f , which is used only once — at the climax of No. 28. Thus it is really a baritone part. Tenors were comparatively rare at this period, and parts in the tenor clef were quite often sung by countertenors or basses. The finest basses had wide ranges, were expected to reach g , and could easily have sung the part of Aeneas. This may therefore have been performed by John Bowman for, although he was one of the principal actors as well as the most prominent bass at the Lincoln's Inn Fields theatre in 1700, he is not included in the cast-list for *Measure for Measure*. The omission suggests that he was singing in the masque. Dido was probably sung by Mrs. Hodgson (or Hudson), since the other main women singers of the company all took part in the play.

Dennis Arundell, noting that most of the scenes of *Dido* are exteriors, has put forward the hypothesis that the work was originally performed out of doors.[25] He speculated that the performance took place not in the grounds of the school building, Gorges House, but in the woodyard of the adjoining Lindsey House, postulating that the nearby Thames would have provided a suitable backdrop for "The Ships"; that the sailors could have roistered in the

23. Edward J. Dent, *Foundations of English Opera* (Cambridge: Cambridge University Press, 1928), p. 192.

24. See the heading of this ode in Purcell's autograph manuscript, British Library RM 20.h.8. Like *Dido and Aeneas* this ode makes little concession to the immaturity of the performers for whom it was written.

25. *The Critic at the Opera* (London: Benn, 1951), pp. 174ff.

adjacent stable yard; and that there was perhaps a tunnel leading from the river to provide the "deep-vaulted cell." There is no evidence for such a tunnel, however, nor would there have been any need for it in this situation. The exploitation of such a setting would have involved considerable movement of the cast to different places and the ground surface would have created difficulties for the dancers. Nor would there have been "natural" settings for all the scenes; some artificial scenery would surely have been necessary. Moreover, the stage directions, "Phoebus rises in the Chariot, over the Sea" and "Venus descends in her Chariot" in the prologue and "Cupids appear in the Clouds o're her Tomb" towards the end of Act III imply the use of quite sophisticated stage machinery. It is noticeable, however, that there is no mention of "sinking" in the 1689 libretto, for this would have required the trapdoors of the professional stage. The rising "out of the Sea" which is specified in the prologue could have been achieved by having "the Sea" sufficiently built up for characters to crouch behind it until needed.

I see no reason why the opera could not have been staged inside Gorges House itself. In 1676, when the building was being used by another girls' school, the occupants staged Duffett's masque *Beauties Triumph*. The descriptions in the printed libretto of the scenery used in the masque make it clear that not only was the performance given inside but also that it took place on a stage able to provide several changes of scene. There must therefore have been a sufficiently large room for such performances, and although the stage may have been specially erected for the occasion, it is possible that some such platform was a permanent feature of the building. In any case, although the performers of *Dido and Aeneas* were amateurs, the man responsible for its production was not. Priest could well have borrowed all the scenery and properties from the Theatre Royal for the required groves, palace, chariots, clouds and so forth, as these were stock items. He may even have secured the assistance of some of the professional machinists. Tate's open-air settings are noteworthy, but they may have been necessitated by the sort of scenery that could be employed on such a stage, which was probably quite small. Little more than back-flats would be needed for most of the scenes, the uncomplicated design leaving plenty of room for dancing. The two Grove scenes were probably identical, possibly with slight variations in moveable properties.

The stage directions given in the libretti are tantalizingly inadequate. The scene change from Sea to Grove in the prologue is complicated by the fact that, contrary to convention, Phoebus and Venus—both apparently in chariots suspended in air, though they may have dismounted before singing—remain on stage during the transformation. The directions give no indication of how this was managed. The Grove Scene opens with Venus and the chorus singing

> See the Spring in all her Glory,
> Welcomes *Venus* to the Shore.

Tate thus presumably intended the change of scene to suggest that Phoebus and Venus were travelling towards "The Grove." The journey may have been indicated purely by the scene-change in the background, but possibly the characters moved from one part of the stage to another as well. Later in the scene the stage direction "Enter the Country Shepherds and Shepherdesses" seems to have been misplaced, since it occurs only after a song and dance for these characters. It is just possible, however, that two separate groups of shepherds were intended, in which case the rubric for the entry of the first set has been omitted altogether.

The staging of Act III is also somewhat problematical. It clearly falls into two sections, the first for the sailors, Sorceress and witches, the second for the courtiers. Although there is no indication in the earlier libretto that the Sorceress and her followers should leave the stage after the Witches' Dance, the "Exeunt" given here in the *Measure for Measure* text is surely correct: they have nothing else to sing, and elsewhere the two groups of characters are kept separate. Neither text is careful about marking the exits, especially at the end of scenes, so this one was probably omitted inadvertently or felt to be unnecessary in the 1689 libretto. The witches' departure would have left an empty stage—the usual marker of the end of a scene—but no scene change is indicated here in the Royal College libretto. The later direction "Cupids appear in the Clouds o're her Tomb," however, suggests that the scene has been changed to allow the tomb to be introduced; moreover, it seems a little unlikely that the Queen's death took place on a public quay. Purcell, too, was careful to provide two bars of held continuo note over which the harpsichordist (probably himself in 1689) is clearly intended to improvise before Dido begins to sing; this implies a new start and would give her entourage time to enter. An indication of a scene-change back to the Palace could have been omitted here, especially since this last page of the Royal College libretto is so cramped, the printer even resorting to smaller type near the end when he realized that the text would not otherwise fit onto an eight-page gathering. No scene-change is indicated here in the *Measure for Measure* text either, but the later libretto is careless about indicating scenes. The scores are no help, since they do not include the scene rubrics at all.

Tate understandably introduced dances into the opera at every possible opportunity, for not only was the work firmly within the masque tradition but

Priest was a dancer and choreographer by profession. Eighteen dances are specified in the Royal College libretto, six in the prologue and twelve in the main opera. The *Measure for Measure* libretto reduces those in the main piece to six and, as we have seen, none of those omitted there are indicated in the scores. The "Dance to entertain Aeneas by Dido Vemon [Women]" required in the 1689 libretto after "Oft she visits" (No. 25) was in all probability performed to the instrumental ritornello which follows the vocal section of this movement. The Cupids' Dance at the end of the work could have been performed either during the final chorus or to an instrumental repeat of it as is usual at the end of Purcell's dramatic operas. It may be relevant that this chorus is marked to be repeated. On the other hand, as Price surmises, the lack of a double bar at the end of this chorus in the Tenbury score may mean that a final dance had been removed.[26] The "Dance for 2 Drunken Sailors" which follows No. 19 in the libretto was probably cut by Purcell himself, for in the scores this movement runs straight into the next. He may well have felt that sailors were incongruous in this scene. Two of the remaining dances in question are a chacony and ground for guitar in Act I and the Grove Scene, respectively. These were no doubt intended to display the talents of one of the girls; the guitar was very popular at the end of the seventeenth century, and Roger North, a knowledgeable amateur, lists it as one of the instruments proper for women.[27] Nevertheless, both these dances seem a little superfluous. It is hardly surprising that they were dropped in 1700; they may never have been provided at all. The remaining omission is "The Baske"; this occurs after the direction "Dance this Cho.," referring to "Fear no danger" (No. 7). These two directions appear to be independent and to call for a Basque dance to be performed directly after the one to "Fear no danger." Two dances in succession, however, seems improbable. The two rubrics may in fact belong together as do "Eccho Dance" and "Inchanteresses and Fairees" at the end of the Cave Scene, although they too are on separate lines. This would mean that the "Fear no danger" dance was intended to be a Basque dance, though its minuet rhythm does not seem entirely suitable. The layout of the Royal College libretto suggests that the "Fear no danger" dance should be performed to an instrumental repeat of the chorus; in the *Measure for Measure* text, however, "Dance this Cho." is placed beside the words for the chorus itself, implying that on that occasion at least the dance was performed while the chorus was being sung. Both procedures occur elsewhere in Purcell, so either is possible; but the fact that Gildon bothered to make the change sug-

26. See above, pp. 38-39.
27. *Roger North on Music*, ed. John Wilson (London: Novello, 1969), p. 16.

gests that there was no separate instrumental version for the dance at this point in the score.

There is no record of any further stage performances of *Dido and Aeneas* after 1706. London taste by then was turning from English dramatic opera towards all-sung opera, mainly in Italian. *Dido* was sung throughout but was not, of course, a complete evening's entertainment by itself; therefore it was probably not staged again.

In the late eighteenth century a concert version was prepared, and some performances seem to have taken place. Three copies of this version are closely related: British Library Add. MS 31450, Add. MS 15979, and Folger Shakespeare Library MS W.b.539.[28] The last two state that they were "copied from a corrected copy in the hands of John Hindle, Mus. Bac., from a corrected copy in the hands of Samuel Howard, Mus. Doc." Add. MS 15979 also bears a note stating that it was copied by Edward Woodley Smith and a date, but unfortunately the last two figures of the year have been cropped in binding. It looks as if the third figure was "9," making the date sometime in the 1790s, presumably after Hindle had gained his Mus. Bac. in 1791.[29] Add MS 31450 is in a very similar hand and contains a virtually identical text. It may be somewhat earlier, since it is preceded by a copy of *The Tempest* made by J. P. Hobler in 1784. It could be either Mr. Hindle's or Dr. Howard's copy. The rubric in Add. MS 15979 suggests that Howard may have been responsible for this version, though it could just mean that he possessed a copy of it. In either case the implication is that it was made before Howard's death in 1782.

In the concert version Belinda (now Anna as in Virgil) becomes a countertenor and the Sorceress a bass. All the dances except the Sailors' Dance are omitted and the continuity destroyed. Many of Purcell's rhythmical figures and ornamental passages are ironed out, and most of the cadences "improved" in accordance with late eighteenth-century taste. String parts are added to No. 11; No. 28 is cut short at bar 15, and the cadence altered to end the movement in B♭ major, the key of the next section. There are sundry other smaller alterations as well.

A collection of parts formerly belonging to Dr. Cummings and now in the Royal Academy of Music (MS 25) also presents this version. The earliest group contains thirty-five vocal and instrumental parts, including ones for two oboes which play in the overture and choruses. One of the chorus bass parts states that it was "completed 22 February 1787." The solo countertenor

28. Gresham Library MS V.I.39 and British Library Add. MS 31451 contain nineteenth-century copies of this concert version.

29. See James D. Brown and Stephen S. Stratton, *British Musical Biography* (London: Reeves, 1897), p. 199.

(Belinda/Anna), tenor (Aeneas) and bass (Sorceress) parts bear the names of Mr. Dyne, Mr. Hindle—presumably the same person who owned the copy score—and Mr. Sale, respectively. Thus the set would seem to have been prepared for a performance in 1787. All the solo items are distributed among the four soloists, who also sang in the choruses, though it is not clear who performed the Second Witch, since both witches' parts are included in the soprano soloist's book. The collection also contains two further single sets of vocal and instrumental parts bearing the dates 1807 and 1817, implying further performances in those years. The 1817 soprano and countertenor parts bear singers' names, and the first violin part has a note about derivation which is identical with that in Add. MS 15979.

The only other notable score of the whole opera is now in the Nanki Library, Tokyo (MS N - 4/41). This contains all the known music, though the first three items have been replaced by a mid-nineteenth-century hand with those of the concert version. From No. 4 onwards, however, the hand is early nineteenth-century and the music appears to have been derived from the Tenbury score or a closely related source. Yet in several places florid passages and cadences have been "improved" in a manner reminiscent of the concert version described above. The Nanki manuscript is therefore an amalgamation of the two versions and cannot be considered a source of primary importance.

Unfortunately, the concert version served as the main source for the first edition of *Dido* published by the Musical Antiquarian Society in 1841 and for all subsequent nineteenth-century editions. Despite the fact that Cummings owned the Nanki score and also had access to the Tenbury manuscript, his edition for the Purcell Society (1889) retained many features of the corrupt concert version, including the bass Sorceress, though he did reinstate all the deleted numbers and restored some of Purcell's characteristic touches. Not until Dent's edition of 1925 was the absolute superiority of the Tenbury version fully recognized.

It is sad that this fascinating and moving work does not survive in its entirety. The paucity of contemporary sources is truly surprising. It is perhaps salutary for us to realize that for Purcell and his contemporaries this little chamber opera was a relatively unimportant work when compared with the more ambitious and sumptuous professional dramatic operas which followed it. Yet it gave Purcell the opportunity to plumb emotional depths which the more fragmented nature of the music in the larger works could not. We can only be thankful that interest in Purcell's music, as evidenced by later manuscript anthologies, recurred at intervals throughout the eighteenth century, and that the scribe of the Tenbury manuscript and, rather later, Philip Hayes, were sufficiently impressed by *Dido and Aeneas* to preserve what they found of it as faithfully as they could.

THE LIBRETTO:
A CRITICAL EDITION

THE LIBRETTO:
A CRITICAL EDITION

The following text is based on the single surviving copy of Nahum Tate's original libretto (hereinafter F1689), now in the Royal College of Music, London. It is an eight-page folio gathering without title-page or printer's name. Orthography, spelling, and italics have been modernized. Textual variants with the so-called *Measure for Measure* libretto (Q1700) and St. Michael's College, Tenbury, MS 1266 (cited simply as Tenbury) are recorded in footnotes. Where the later two sources agree and are different from Tate's libretto, the majority reading is normally adopted, while that in F1689 is treated as a variant.

The Prologue[1]

Phoebus *rises in the chariot, over the sea, the* Nereids *out of the sea.*[2]

PHOEBUS.	From Aurora's spicy bed,	
	Phoebus rears his sacred head.[3]	
	His coursers advancing,	
	Curvetting and prancing.	
1ST NEREID.	Phoebus strives in vain to tame 'em,[4]	**5**
	With Ambrosia[5] fed too high.	
2ND NEREID.	Phoebus ought not now to blame 'em,	
	Wild and eager to survey	
	The fairest pageant of the sea.	
PHOEBUS.	Tritons and Nereids come pay your devotion	**10**
CHORUS.	To the new rising star of the ocean.	

1. No music survives for the prologue. For a discussion of whether Purcell ever set it, see pp. 15-19, 48-53, and 250-52.
2. Nautical symbols and imagery had long been applied to the British monarch, whom Phoebus probably represented. See, for example, *The Works of John Dryden* (Berkeley and Los Angeles: University of California Press, 1956-), XV, ed. Earl Miner et al., 327-9.
3. "Sacred," that is consecrated, as at a coronation.
4. Implies that Phoebus, who symbolizes William III, is not yet in complete control.
5. The fabled elixir of life.

Venus *descends in her chariot, the* Tritons *out of the sea.*[6] *The* Tritons *dance.*

[*1ST*] *NEREID.*	Look down ye orbs and see
	A new divinity.[7]
PHOEBUS.	Whose lustre does outshine
	Your fainter beams, and half eclipses mine,[8]

15

	Give Phoebus leave to prophesy.
	Phoebus all events can see.
	Ten thousand thousand harms,
	From such prevailing charms,
	To gods and men must instantly ensue.[9]

20

CHORUS.	And if the deities above
	Are victims of the powers of Love,
	What must wretched mortals do[?]
VENUS.	Fear not, Phoebus, fear not me,
	A harmless deity.

25

	These are all my guards ye view,
	What can these blind archers[10] do[?]
PHOEBUS.	Blind they are, but strike the heart.
VENUS.	What Phoebus says is always true.
	They wound indeed, but 'tis a pleasing smart.

30

PHOEBUS.	Earth and skies address their duty,
	To the sovereign queen of beauty.
	All resigning,
	None repining
	At her undisputed sway.

35

CHORUS.	To Phoebus and Venus our homage we'll pay,
	Her charms blessed the night, as his beams blessed[11]
	the day.

6. Q1700: the Tritons rise out of the Sea. See above, pp. 54–55.

7. Venus probably represents Mary II, who arrived in England in early 1689, shortly after her husband.

8. William and Mary were co-monarchs in state, but the former was head of administration. Throughout the prologue Phoebus and Venus are treated as equals.

9. The threat is from Venus's beauty, not from the new political order her entrance represents. The choice of Venus as protagonist was felicitous, because in sixteenth- and seventeenth-century British political mythology, the goddess had adopted Britain as her new home. Consider, for example, "Fairest isle" in Dryden's *King Arthur*: "Venus here will choose her dwelling, / And forsake her Cyprian grove."

10. That is, little Cupids, who ironically reappear at the end of Act III to scatter roses on Dido's tomb.

11. Q1700: bless the night . . . bless the day.

The Nereids *Dance.*　　　　　　　　　　　　　　　　*Exit.*

Scene [ii]: *the Grove. The* Spring *Enters with her nymphs.*[12]

VENUS.	See the Spring in all her glory,
CHORUS.	Welcomes Venus to the shore.
VENUS.	Smiling hours are now before you,　　　　**40**
	Hours that may return no more.[13]

Exit Phoebus [*and*] Venus.[14] *Soft music.*[15]

SPRING.	Our youth and form declare,
	For what we were designed.
	'Twas Nature made us fair,
	And you must make us kind.[16]　　　　**45**
	He that fails of addressing,
	'Tis but just he should fail of possessing.

The Spring *and nymphs dance.*
Enter shepherds and shepherdesses.

SHEPHERDESSES.	Jolly shepherds come away,
	To celebrate this genial day,
	And take the friendly hours you vow to pay.　　**50**
	Now make trial,
	And take no denial.
	Now carry your game, or forever give o're.

The shepherds and shepherdesses dance.

CHORUS.	Let us love and happy live,
	Possess those smiling hours,　　　　**55**
	The more auspicious powers,
	And gentle planets give.
	Prepare those soft returns to meet,
	That makes Love's[17] torments sweet.

　　12. Q1700: The Scene changes to a Grove. The Spring appears in an Arbour, with her Nymphs about her.
　　13. An allusion both to the following tragedy and to the fleeting youth of the performers.
　　14. The protagonists abruptly depart in the midst of the entertainment offered in their honor. For the probable reason, see p. 53.
　　15. For the conclusion of this scene as given in Q1700, see pp. 77-78.
　　16. Spring addresses the audience.
　　17. Q1700: Love.

The nymphs dance. Enter the country shepherds and shepherdesses.

HE.	Tell, tell me, prithee Dolly,	**60**
	And leave thy melancholy,	
	Why on the plains, the nymphs and swains,	
	This morning are so jolly[?]	
SHE.	By Zephyr's gentle blowing,	
	And Venus' graces flowing,[18]	**65**
	The sun has been to court our queen,[19]	
	And tired the Spring with wooing.	
HE.	The sun does gild our bowers,	
SHE.	The Spring does yield us flowers.	
	She sends the vine,	**70**
HE.	He makes the wine,	
	To charm our happy hours.	
SHE.	She gives our flocks their feeding,	
HE.	He makes 'em fit for breeding.	
SHE.	She decks the plain,	**75**
HE.	He fills the grain,	
	And makes it worth the weeding.	
CHORUS.	But the jolly nymph Thitis[20] that long his love sought,	
	Has flustered him now with a large morning's draught.	
	Let's go and divert him, whilst he is mellow,	**80**
	You know in his cups he's a hot-headed fellow.	

The country maids[21] *dance.*

Act the First

Scene the Palace. Enter Dido *and* Belinda, *and Train.*[1]

BELINDA.	Shake the cloud from off your brow,	
	Fate your wishes does[2] allow.	

18. Q1700: And Grace of Venus flowing.
19. The innocent country girl confirms that Venus is her sovereign, thereby strengthening the link with Queen Mary.
20. Q1700 renders this "Thetis." The chorus is a *non sequitur.* Thitis is apparently not the same as Dolly mentioned in line 60 above.
21. F1689 has "Countreys Maids."
1. Q1700: The *Loves* of *Dido* and *Aeneas*, a Mask, in Four Musical Entertainments. *The First* Entertainment. *Enter* QUEEN DIDO, Belinda, *and* Train.
2. F1689: do.

	Empire growing,	
	Pleasures flowing	
	Fortune smiles and so should you,	5
	Shake the cloud from off your brow.	
CHORUS.	Banish sorrow, banish care.	
	Grief[3] should ne're approach the fair.	
DIDO.	Ah! Belinda I am press'd,	
	With torment not to be confess'd.	10
	Peace and I are strangers grown,	
	I languish till my grief is known,	
	Yet would not have it guess'd.	
BELINDA.	Grief increasing,[4] by concealing,	
DIDO.	Mine admits of no revealing.	15
BELINDA.	Then let me speak, the Trojan guest,	
	Into your tender thoughts has press'd.	
2ND WOMAN.[5]	The greatest blessing Fate can give,	
	Our Carthage to secure, and Troy revive.	
CHORUS.	When monarchs unite,[6] how happy their state,	20
	They triumph at once o're[7] their foes and their fate.	
DIDO.	Whence could so much virtue spring,	
	What storms, what battles did he sing[?]	
	Anchises' valour mix'd with Venus' charms,[8]	
	How soft in peace, and yet how fierce in arms.[9]	25
BELINDA.	A tale so strong and full of woe,	
	Might melt the rocks as well as you.	
2ND WOMAN.[10]	What stubborn heart unmoved could see,	
	Such distress, such pity[?][11]	

3. Virgil's Dido is in mourning for her late husband, Sychaeus; see above, p. 12.
4. There appears to be no authority for the Purcell Society edition's "increases."
5. F1689: 2 Women; Q1700: 2 Woman; for an explication, see above, p. 51.
6. This continues the theme of co-reigning begun in the prologue; see above, pp. 6–7.
7. F1689: on.
8. Dardan Anchises was Aeneas's father, Venus his mother.
9. Compare the opening lines of Dryden's translation of the *Aeneid*:

> Arms, and the Man I sing, who, forc'd by Fate,
> And haughty *Juno*'s unrelenting Hate;
> Expell'd and exil'd, left the *Trojan* Shoar . . .

10. See note 5, above.
11. Tenbury: piety.

DIDO.	Mine with storms of care oppress'd,	30
	Is taught to pity[12] the distress'd.[13]	
	Mean wretches grief can touch,	
	So soft so sensible my breast,	
	But ah! I fear, I pity his too much.	
BELINDA.	Fear no danger to ensue,	35
2ND WOMAN.[14]	The hero loves as well as you.	
CHORUS.[15]	Ever gentle, ever smiling,	
	And the cares of life beguiling.	
	Cupids[16] strew your path with flowers,	
	Gathered from Elizian bowers.	40

Dance this Cho.: The Baske.[17]
Aeneas *enters with his train.*[18]

BELINDA.	See your royal guest appears,	
	How god-like is the form he bears.	
AENEAS.	When royal fair shall I be bless'd,	
	With cares of love, and state distress'd[?]	
DIDO.	Fate forbids what you pursue,[19]	45
AENEAS.[20]	Aeneas has no fate but you.	
	Let Dido smile, and I'll defy	
	The feeble stroke of Destiny.	
CHORUS.	Cupid only throws the dart,	
	That's dreadful to a warrior's heart.	50
	And she that wounds can only cure the smart.	
AENEAS.	If not for mine, for empire's sake,	
	Some pity on your lover take.	
	Ah! make not in a hopeless fire,	
	A hero fall, and Troy once more expire.[21]	55

12. Q1700: to wtihout [*sic*].

13. Compare the similar lines in Dryden's *Albion and Albanius* (1685), III.i.15–16: "Un-helpt I am, who pity'd the distress'd, / And none oppressing, am by all oppress'd."

14. Q1700: lines 35–6 given to Belinda; Tenbury: lines 35–6 are a duet for Belinda and the Second Woman.

15. Q1700: Dance to this Cho. [in right margin opposite lines 37–8]; see above, pp. 56–58.

16. F1689: Cupid's.

17. Q1700: omits this stage direction.

18. Q1700: *Enter* Aeneas *with his* Train.

19. F1689: ensue.

20. F1689: lacks speech-prefix.

21. F1689: empire. Probably a printer's error, unless the couplet is interpreted thus: if you do not grant my wish, I will sail on to my destiny of building a new Trojan empire.

BELINDA.   Pursue thy conquest, Love — her Eyes
                   Confess the flame her tongue denies.

     *A dance guitar's chacony.*²²

CHORUS.   To the hills and the vales, to the rocks and the
                        mountains
                   To the musical groves, and the cool shady fountains.
                   Let the triumphs of Love and of beauty be shown,   **60**
                   Go revel ye Cupids, the day is your own.

     The Triumphing Dance.

Act the Second
[Scene i]

     *Scene the Cave.*¹ *Enter* Sorceress.²

SORCERESS.   Wayward³ sisters you that fright
                   The lonely traveller by night.
                   Who like dismal ravens crying,
                   Beat the windows of the dying.
                   Appear at my call, and share in the fame   **5**
                   Of a mischief shall make all Carthage flame.⁴

     *Enter enchantresses.*⁵

ENCHANTRESS.⁶   Say beldame what's thy will?
                   Harm's our delight and mischief all our skill.⁷
SORCERESS.   The Queen of Carthage, whom we hate,
                   As we do all in prosperous state.   **10**
                   Ere sun-set shall most wretched prove,
                   Deprived of fame, of life and love.
CHORUS.   Ho, ho, ho, ho, ho, ho, &c.

---

    22. Omitted in both Q1700 and Tenbury.
    1. In Q1700 this scene follows the Grove (Act II, scene ii); in Tenbury this is the second
scene of Act I.
    2. Q1700: *The* SCENE *the* Cave *Rises. The* Witches *appear.*
    3. Q1700: Weyward.
    4. F1689: Carthage to flame.
    5. Q1700: *Enter* Witches.
    6. Q1700: Witch; Tenbury: 1ˢᵗ Witch.
    7. Q1700 and Tenbury: line 8 given to the chorus.

ENCHANTRESS.[8]	Ruin'd ere the set of sun,
	Tell us how shall this be done?[9] **15**
SORCERESS.	The Trojan Prince you know is bound
	By Fate to seek Italian ground.[10]
	The Queen and he are now in chase,
	Hark, how the cry comes on apace.[11]
	But when they've done, my trusty elf **20**
	In form of Mercury himself,
	As sent from Jove shall chide his stay,
	And charge him sail tonight with all his fleet away.
CHORUS.[12]	Ho, ho, ho, ho, &c.

Enter 2 drunken sailors, a dance.[13]

SORCERESS.[14]	But ere we this perform,[15] **25**
	We'll conjure for a storm
	To mar their hunting sport,
	And drive 'em back to court.
CHORUS.[16]	In our deep-vaulted cell the charm we'll prepare,
	Too dreadful a practice for this open air. **30**

Echo Dance. Enchantresses and Fairies.[17]

[Scene ii][18]

Enter Aeneas, Dido *and* Belinda, *and their Train. Scene the Grove.*[19]

BELINDA.	Thanks to these lovesome[20] vales,
	These desert hills and dales.

8. Q1700: Witch; Tenbury: 1st Witch.
9. Tenbury: line 15 sung by 1st and 2nd Witch.
10. That is, to refound Troy on the banks of the Tiber River.
11. Q1700 and Tenbury omit "how". Tenbury gives line 19 to 1st Witch.
12. F1689 omits speech-prefix.
13. Stage direction omitted from Q1700 and Tenbury.
14. Q1700:.Sorceress and Witch; Tenbury: duet for 1st and 2nd Witches.
15. F1689: But ere we, we this perform.
16. Q1700: "Eccho" replaces speech-prefix; Tenbury: Chorus in a Manner of an Echo.
17. Q1700: Eccho Dance of Furies. *At the end of the Dance Six* Furies *Sinks* [sic]. *The four open the Cave fly up*; Tenbury: Thunder & Lightning horrid Musick. The Furies sink down in the Cave the Rest fly up. The End of the first Part.
18. Here begins Act II in Tenbury.
19. Q1700: omits stage direction.
20. Tenbury: lonesome.

So fair the game, so rich the sport,
Diana's self might to these woods resort.[21]

Guitar ground a dance.[22]

2ND WOMAN.[23]	Oft she visits this loved[24] mountain,	**35**
	Oft she bathes her in this fountain.	
	Here Actaeon met his fate,	
	Pursued by his own hounds,	
	And after mortal wounds	
	Discovered, discovered too late.[25]	**40**

A dance to entertain Aeneas, *by* Dido's *women.*[26]

AENEAS.	Behold upon my bending spear,	
	A monster's head stands bleeding,	
	With tushes[27] far exceeding	
	Those[28] did Venus' huntsmen tear.	
DIDO.	The skies are clouded, hark, how thunder[29]	**45**
	Rends the mountain oaks asunder.	
	Haste, haste to town[;] this open field	
	No shelter from the storm can yield.[30]	

Exit.[31]

The spirit of the Sorceress[32] *descends to* Aeneas *in likeness of* Mercury.

SPIRIT.	Stay Prince and hear great Jove's command,	
	He summons thee this night away.	**50**
AENEAS.	Tonight?	
SPIRIT.	Tonight thou must forsake this land,	

21. F1689: lines 32-4 given to chorus; Q1700: Repeat this Cho. [referring to lines 33-4].
22. Q1700 and Tenbury omit stage direction.
23. F1689 gives "2ᵈ· Wom." Cf. Act I, note 5.
24. Q1700: lov'd; Tenbury: lone.
25. Q1700: too too late. For the relevance of the story of Diana and Actaeon, see above, p. 29.
26. F1689: by Dido Vemon; Q1700 omits stage direction.
27. That is, tusks.
28. F1689: these.
29. Q1700 has stage direction "Thunder."
30. Tenbury: lines 47-8 given to Belinda, then repeated by the chorus.
31. F1689 does not use "Exeunt" here or elsewhere, so the lack of the plural command does not necessarily mean that only Dido leaves the stage.
32. That is, the "trusty elf" mentioned in II.i.20, above, not the Sorceress herself.

               The angry god will brook no longer stay,[33]

               Jove[34] commands thee waste no more

               In love's delights those precious hours,   **55**

               Allowed by the almighty[35] powers,

               To gain th'Hesperian[36] shore

               And ruined Troy restore.

AENEAS.   Jove's commands shall be obeyed

               Tonight our anchors shall be weighed,   **60**

               But ah![37] what language can I try,

               My injured Queen to pacify?

               No sooner she resigns her heart,

               But from her arms I'm forced to part.

               How can so hard a fate be took,   **65**

               One night enjoyed, the next forsook?[38]

               Yours[39] be the blame, ye gods, for I

               Obey your will — but with more ease could die.[40]

The Sorceress *and her enchantresses.*[41]

CHORUS.   Then since our charms have sped,

               A merry dance be led   **70**

               By the nymphs of Carthage to please us.

               They shall all dance to ease us.

               A dance that shall make the spheres to wonder,

               Rending those fair groves asunder.

The Grove's dance.

---

33. In other words, Jove will permit you to stay in Carthage no longer.

34. F1689: Joves.

35. Tenbury: th'almighty.

36. Q1700: the Hesperian [that is, western].

37. Q1700: But ha!

38. Tate's preference for the archaic past participle was common in the late seventeenth century and should not be regarded as a sign of poetastery.

39. F1689: Your.

40. For the continuation of this scene in Q1700, see pp. 78–79. The problem of the missing music is discussed on pp. 15–21.

41. Q1700: *Enter* Sorceress *and* Witches.

Act the Third

Scene the Ships. Enter the sailors. The Sorceress *and her enchantresses.*[1]

1ST SAILOR.[2]	Come away, fellow sailors, your anchors be
	weighing,
	Time and tide will admit no delaying.
	Take a bouze[3] short leave of your nymphs on the
	shore,[4]
	And silence their mourning
	With vows of returning,
	But never intending to visit them more.[5]

The sailors dance.[6]

SORCERESS.	See the flags and streamers curling,
	Anchors weighing, sails unfurling.
	Phoebus' pale deluding beams,[7]
	Gilding more[8] deceitful streams.[9]
	Our plot has took
	The Queen[10] forsook, ho, ho, ho.
	Elisa's ruin'd, ho, ho, ho.[11]
	Our next Motion
	Must be to storm her lover on the ocean.
	From the ruins[12] of others our pleasure we borrow,
	Elisa[13] bleeds tonight, and Carthage flames
	tomorrow.

The line numbers in the right margin read: 5 (at "With vows of returning,"), 10 (at "Gilding more deceitful streams."), 15 (at "Must be to storm her lover on the ocean.").

1. Q1700: Enter Sorceress and Witches. Enter Saylors; Tenbury delays the entrance of the Sorceress until after line 6.
2. F1689: Cho.; Q1700: Sorc. For a discussion of who should sing this song, see pp. 31–32.
3. Tenbury: bouzy.
4. Q1700: Take a Bouze short; leave your Nymphs. . . . The play-book compositor obviously misunderstood this line, though few singers ever have.
5. Tenbury: lines 1–6 repeated by chorus.
6. Tenbury: Enter Sorceress & Witches.
7. Given Phoebus's symbolic function in the prologue, this allusion would seem misguided, unless the intention was to link the god with the witches' deceit.
8. Tenbury: o'er. This line may have an ironic connection to the prologue, line 68.
9. Tenbury: lines 9–10 are sung by 1st Witch.
10. Tenbury: Queen's.
11. Tenbury: lines 11–13 sung as a duet for the 1st Witch and an unnamed character, either another witch or the Sorceress herself. Both F1689 and Q1700 run lines 13 and 14 together, omitting the word "Our"; Tenbury reads "Elisza."
12. Tenbury: ruin.
13. F1689: Elisas.

CHORUS.   Destruction[14] our delight, delight our greatest
                               sorrow,
                        Elisa[15] dies tonight, and Carthage flames tomorrow.

Jack *of the Lanthorn leads the* Spaniards *out of their way among the
enchantresses. A dance.*[16]
Enter Dido, Belinda, *and train.*[17]

DIDO.   Your counsel all is urged in vain,   **20**
                        To earth and heaven I will complain.
                        To earth and heaven why do I call?
                        Earth and heaven conspire my fall.
                        To fate I sue, of other means bereft,
                        The only refuge for the wretched left.[18]   **25**
BELINDA.   See, madam, where the Prince appears,
                        Such sorrow in his looks he bears,

        Aeneas *enters.*

                        As would convince you still he's true.
AENEAS.[19]   What shall lost Aeneas do?
                        How, royal fair, shall I impart   **30**
                        The gods'[20] decree and tell you we must part[?]
DIDO.   Thus on the fatal banks of Nile,
                        Weeps the deceitful crocodile.
                        Thus hypocrites that murder act,
                        Make heaven and gods the authors of the fact.   **35**
AENEAS.   By all that's good,
DIDO.   By all that's good no more,
                        All that's good you have forswore.[21]
                        To your promised empire fly,
                        And let forsaken Dido die.
AENEAS.   In spite of Jove's command I'll stay,[22]

---

14. Tenbury: Destruction's.
15. See note 13 above.
16. Q1700: A Dance of Wizards and Witches. Exeunt; Tenbury: The Witches Dance. For a discussion of this dance, see pp. 32–33.
17. Q1700: Enter Queen *Dido*, Belinda. . .
18. Q1700: Enter *Aeneas* (after line 25).
19. F1689 places this speech-prefix a line too soon.
20. Without apostrophe in any source; thus, Aeneas could mean "the god's decree," that is, the message from the false Mercury.
21. F1689: forsworn.
22. F1689: I stay.

Offend the gods, and love[23] obey.

DIDO. No, faithless man, thy course pursue,
I'm now resolved as well as you.
No repentance shall reclaim 45
The injured Dido's[24] slighted flame.
For 'tis enough whate'er you now decree,
That you had once a thought of leaving me.

AENEAS. Let Jove say what he will,[25] I'll stay.[26]

DIDO. Away[!] 50

Exit Aeneas.

To death I'll fly, if longer you delay.
But death, alas,[27] I cannot shun,
Death must come when he is gone.

CHORUS. Great minds against themselves conspire,
And shun the cure they most desire. 55

DIDO. Thy hand Belinda, darkness shades me,
On thy bosom let me rest.

Cupids *appear in the clouds o'er her tomb.*[28]

More I would but death invades me.
Death is now a welcome guest.
When I am laid in earth may[29] my wrongs create 60
No trouble in thy breast,
Remember me, but ah! forget my fate.

CHORUS. With drooping wings you Cupids come
To scatter roses on her tomb.[30]
Soft and gentle as her heart,
Keep here your watch and never part.

Cupids *dance.*[31]

FINIS

23. All sources have "Love", that is, Cupid, which would make nonsense of this line.
24. F1689: Dido.
25. Tenbury: please.
26. In Tenbury line 49 is expanded to "I'll stay, no, no, I'll stay and Love obey," forming a duet with Dido, line 51.
27. F1689: alas? [the question mark is probably a misreading of "alas!"].
28. This stage direction, not found in Q1700 or Tenbury, is placed to the right of lines 56–7 in F1689.
29. F1689: in Earth my wrongs.
30. Q1700: line 64 omitted; for the possible reason, see above, pp. 39–41.
31. Q1700 and Tenbury omit dance.

The Epilogue[1]

All that we know the angels do above,
I've read, is that they sing and that they love,
The vocal part we have tonight perform'd
And if by Love our hearts not yet are warm'd
Great Providence has still more bounteous been   5
To save us from these grand deceivers, men.
Here blest with innocence, and peace of mind,
Not only bred to virtue, but inclin'd;
We flourish, and defy all human kind.[2]
Art's curious garden thus we learn to know,   10
And here secure from nipping blasts we grow,
Let the vain fop range o'er yon vile lewd town,
Learn play-house wit, and vow 'tis all his own;
Let him cock, huff, strut, ogle, lie, and swear
How he's admir'd by such and such a player;   15
All's one to us, his charms have here no power,
Our hearts have just the temper as before;
Besides, to show we live with strictest rules,
Our nunnery-door is charm'd to shut out fools;
No love-toy here can pass to private view,   20
Nor China orange cramm'd with billet doux,
Rome may allow strange tricks to please her sons,[3]
But we are Protestants and English nuns;
Like nimble fawns, and birds that bless the spring
Unscarr'd by turning times we dance and sing;   25
We hope to please, but if some critic here
Fond of his wit, designs to be severe,
Let not his patience be worn out too soon;
In a few years we shall be all in tune.

1. By Thomas Durfey. This first appeared in his *New Poems* (1689): "Epilogue to the Opera of Dido and Aeneas, perform'd at Mr. Preist's Boarding School at Chelsey; Spoken by the Lady Dorothy Burk." Durfey was a popular playwright and an indefatigable lyricist who had collaborated with Purcell on the comedy *A Fool's Preferment*, which has its premiere in April 1689, almost exactly a year before *Dido and Aeneas*.

2. This may be satirical. Compare the behavior of the young girls depicted in Durfey's comedy *Love for Money; or, the Boarding School* (1691).

3. See above, p. 45 and below, p. 229. Lines 21 and 22 should probably be read as parts of the same idea: that is, the smuggling of love letters in a China orange is not unlike the substitution of a healthy baby for a still-born one, as was alleged to have happened with the aid of a warming pan when Mary of Modena presented James II with a Catholic heir to the throne on 10 June 1688, thereby triggering the Glorious Revolution.

Gildon's Conclusion of the Prologue (1700)*

Enter Mars and his attendants, on one side, *Peace* and her train on the other.[1]

MARS.	Bid the warlike trumpet sound,
	Conquest waits with laurel crown'd,
	Conquest is the hero's due,
	Glorious triumph will ensue.
PEACE.	'Tis time for war's alarms to cease, **5**
	And heroes crown'd with spoils,
	Enjoy the harvest of their toils,
	And reap the happy fruits of Peace.

MARS AND HIS
TRAIN (CHORUS).   No, no! though Love would have it so.
                  Fame and Honour answer—No.   **10**

PEACE.	Wherefore must the warrior be
	To restless tasks assign'd[?]
	Give others those delights which he
	Must never hope to find,
	Shall he, whose valour gain'd **15**
	The prize in rough alarms,
	Be still condemn'd to arms,
	And from a victor's share detain'd[?]

MARS AND	
CHORUS.	Yes, yes.
PEACE AND	
CHORUS.	No, no. **20**
MARS AND	
CHORUS.	Fame, Fame will have it so.
PEACE AND	
CHORUS.	Love and reason answer no.
PEACE.	Must he with endless toils be press'd,
	Nor with repose himself be bless'd,
	Who gives the weary nations rest[?] **25**

---

*Charles Gildon, *Measure for Measure* (London: D. Brown, 1700), pp. 46–[48].
1. Spring's song and the entry for shepherds (prologue, lines 42–59) are placed after the rustic dialogue (lines 60–81).

MARS AND	
CHORUS.	Yes, yes.
PEACE AND	
CHORUS.	No, no.
ALL.	Love, reason, honour, all will have it so.
CHORUS.	Since it is decreed that wars should cease,
	Let's all agree to welcome Peace. 30

The grand dance.

*Gildon's Insertion for the Grove Scene (1700)**

[AENEAS].	"Direct me, friends, what choice to make,	
	"Since Love and Fame together press me,	
	"And with equal force distress me.	
	"Say what party I shall take[?][1]	
1ST FRIEND.[2]	Resistless Jove commands—	5
2ND FRIEND.	But Love	
	More resistless than[3] Jove's.	
AENEAS.	But fame, Alcander.	
2ND FRIEND.	Fame's a bubble,	
	Honour but a glorious trouble,	10
	A vain pride of destroying,	
	Alarming and arming,	
	And toiling and moiling,	
	And never enjoying.	
1ST FRIEND.	'Twas that gave Hector,	15
2ND FRIEND.	What?	
1ST FRIEND.	Renown and fame.	
2ND FRIEND.	An empty name,	
	And lamentable fate.	
1ST FRIEND.	'Twas noble and brave.	20

*Gildon, Measure for Measure, pp. 14–15.

1. The quotation marks at the left margin show that these four lines were omitted during the performance.

2. Q1700: 1 Fr. 2 Fr.

3. Q1700: then.

2ND FRIEND.	'Twas a death for a slave.
1ST FRIEND.	His valour and glory,
	Shall flourish in story.
2ND FRIEND.	While he rots in his grave.
AENEAS.	Ye sacred powers instruct me how to choose, 　25
	When Love or Empire I must loose.
AENEAS AND	
CHORUS.	Love with Empire trifling is but vain,
	And Empire without Love a pompous pain.

　　　Exeunt.[4]

　　4. The scene continues as in Tate, II.ii.69-74.

THE SCORE

The Purcell Society Score which follows was edited by Margaret Laurie and Thurston Dart and is reproduced by permission of the publisher, Novello & Co., Ltd.

The following emendations to the score were made by the editors:
notes, ornaments, and accidentals in small type
square-bracketed material
tempo marks in italics
rhythm heads above staves
regroupings of bars in the continuo part.

Dramatis Personae

DIDO, or ELISSA, Queen of Carthage	Soprano
BELINDA, her sister	Soprano
SECOND WOMAN	Soprano
SORCERESS	Mezzo-Soprano
FIRST WITCH	Soprano
SECOND WITCH	Soprano
SPIRIT	Mezzo-Soprano
AENEAS, a Trojan Prince	Tenor
SAILOR	Soprano (or Tenor)

Chorus (with Dancers) of Courtiers, Witches, etc.

INSTRUMENTATION

Violin I
Violin II
Viola
Violoncello
 Basso Continuo
Harpsichord

1 OVERTURE

ACT I

{SCENE – The Palace} *Enter Dido, Belinda and attendants*

87

I   are stran - gers grown,   Peace and I   are   stran - gers, stran - gers

RITOR.
Violin I

Violin II

Viola

grown.

DIDO

stub-born heart un-mov'd____ could see Such dis-tress, such pi - e-ty? Mine with

storms _____ of care ____ opp-press'd Is taught to pi - ty the dis-

tress'd; Mean wretch-es' grief can touch, So soft, so sen-si-ble my

breast, But ah!_ but ah! I fear I pi-ty his too_ much.

Allegro

Ev-er gen - tle, ev-er smil-ing, And the cares of life be - guil - ing.

Ev-er gen - tle, ev-er smil-ing, And the cares of life be - guil - ing.

[p]

Fear no dan - ger to en - sue, The he - ro loves as well as you.

Fear no dan - ger to en - sue, The he - ro loves as well as you.

Fear no dan - ger to en - sue, The he - ro loves as well as you.

Fear no dan - ger to en - sue, The he - ro loves as well as you.

f

Cu - pids strew your paths with flowers, Ga-ther'd from E - ly - sian bowers.

Cu - pids strew your paths with flowers, Ga-ther'd from E - ly - sian bowers.

[*p*]

Fear no dan - ger to en - sue, The he -ro loves as well as you.

Fear no dan - ger to en - sue, The he -ro loves as well as you.

Fear no dan - ger to en - sue, The he - ro loves as well as you.

Fear no dan - ger to en - sue, The he - ro loves as well as you.

Cu - pid on - ly throws the_ dart That's dread - ful to a war - rior's heart, That's

dread - ful, Cu - pid on - ly throws_ the dart, on - ly throws the dart, That's

Cu - pid on - ly throws the dart _____ That's

throws the dart That's dread - ful, dread - ful, Cu - pid on - ly throws the dart That's

dread - ful to a war - rior's heart, And she that wounds, and she that wounds can

dread - ful to ___ a war - rior's heart, And she that wounds, and she that wounds can

dread - ful to a war - rior's heart, And she that wounds, and she that wounds can

dread - ful to a war - rior's heart, And she that wounds, and she that wounds can

- umphs of love and of beau - ty be shown.

tri-umphs of love and of beau - ty be shown.

tri-umphs of love and of beau - ty be shown.

- umphs of love and of beau - ty be shown.

beau - ty be shown. To the hills and the vales, to the rocks and the moun-tains, To the mu-si-cal_

beau - ty be shown. To the hills and the vales, to the rocks and the moun-tains, To the mu - si - cal

beau - ty be shown. To the hills and the vales, to the rocks and the moun-tains, To the mu - si - cal

beau - ty be shown. To the hills and the vales, to the rocks and the moun-tains, To the mu - si - cal

groves and the cool sha - dy foun - tains Let the tri - - umphs, let the

groves and the cool sha - dy foun - tains Let the tri - umphs, the tri - -

groves and the cool sha - dy foun - tains Let the tri - umphs, let the

groves and the cool sha - dy foun - tains Let the tri - umphs, let the tri - umphs, the

Cu - pids, go re - vel, go re - vel ye Cu - pids, go re - vel, the day is your own.

re - vel ye Cu - pids, go re - vel, go re - vel ye Cu - pids, the day is your own.

re - vel, go re - vel ye Cu - pids, go re - vel ye Cu - pids, the day is your own.

Cu - pids, go re - vel, go re - vel, go re - vel ye Cu - pids, the day is your own.

segue

13 The Triumphing Dance

L'istesso tempo

Act I

ACT II

SCENE I

{SCENE – The Cave. *Enter Sorceress.*}

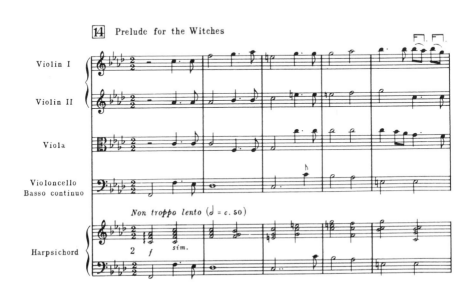

dy - ing, Ap - pear! Ap-pear at my call, and share in the fame Of a

mis - chief shall make all___ Car - thage flame. Ap - pear! Ap -

Enter WITCHES

1st WITCH

pear! Ap-pear! Ap-pear! Say, Bel-dame, say, what's thy will?

and mis - chief, mis - chief all our skill.

skill, and mis - chief, mis - chief all our skill.

mis - chief, mis - chief, mis - chief all our skill.

all___ our skill, and mis - chief all our skill.

16

SORCERESS

The Queen of Car-thage, whom we hate, As we do all in_pros-p'rous state, Ere

Non troppo lento

done,   my trus-ty   elf,___ In form of Mer-cu-ry   him-self,   As sent from Jove, shall

CHORUS chide his stay, And   charge him sail to-night___ with all his fleet a - way!

SOPRANO

ALTO

Ho ho   ho ho ho

TENOR

BASS

Ho ho

Thunder and lightning, horrid music. The Furies sink down in the cave, the rest fly up.

ACT II
SCENE II

24 {SCENE— The Grove}. *Enter Aeneas, Dido, Belinda and their train.*

ter mor - tal_ wounds Dis - cov - - er'd too, too late; And af - ter,

af - ter_ mor - - tal wounds Dis - cov - er'd too, too late; Here Ac-

{A Dance to entertain Aeneas by Dido's women}

RITOR.

Violin I

Violin II

Viola

tae - on_ met his fate.

27

BELINDA

Haste, haste to town, haste, haste, haste, haste, haste ___ to town, haste, haste to town! this o-pen field No

shel -ter, this o-pen field No shel -ter from the storm, ___ the storm can yield; Haste, haste,

haste, haste, haste to town, haste, haste ___ to_town, haste, haste, haste, haste, haste, haste ___

shel - ter from the storm, _____ the storm can yield; Haste, haste, haste, haste to town, haste,

o - pen field No shel-ter from the storm, the storm can yield; Haste, haste to town, haste, haste, haste, haste to

shel - ter from the storm, _____ the storm can yield; Haste, haste, haste, haste to town, haste,

o - pen field No shel-ter from the storm _____ can yield; Haste, haste, haste, haste to

f   *p*   *mf*

haste ___ to _ town, haste, haste, haste, haste, haste, haste, haste _____ to _ town!

town, haste, haste to town, haste, haste, haste, haste, haste, haste, haste, haste ___ to town!

haste ___ to town, haste, haste, haste, haste, haste, haste, haste, haste to town!

town, haste, haste, haste, haste, haste, haste, haste, haste, haste, haste to town!

28 *The Spirit of the Sorceress descends to Aeneas in the likeness of Mercury*

SPIRIT   AENEAS   SPIRIT

Stay, Prince, and hear great Jove's com-mand: He sum-mons thee this night a - way.   To-night? To-

night thou must for-sake this land; The an-gry god will brook no long-er stay. Jove com-

mands thee, waste no more In love's de-lights those pre-cious hours Al-low'd by th' al-might-y powers To gain

__th' Hes-pe-rian shore And ru-in'd Troy re-store. Jove's com-mands shall be o-bey'd; To-

AENEAS

night our an-chors shall be weigh'd. But ah! _____ but ah!

ACT III

{SCENE [I] – The Ships}

153

more,   no   nev-er,   no   nev-er   in - tend-ing to__   vis - it them

more!

CHORUS

SOPRANO

Come a - way,   fel - low sai - lors, come a - way, Your

ALTO

Come a - way,   fel - low sai - lors, come a - way,   come a - way,   come a - way, Your

TENOR

Come a - way,   fel - low sai - lors, come a - way,   come a - way, Your

BASS

Come a - way,   fel - low sai - lors, come a - way,   come a - way,   come a - way, Your

leave   of your nymphs of   the   shore,   And   si - lence their mourn-ing With   vows of   re -

leave   of your nymphs of   the   shore,   And   si - lence their mourn-ing With   vows of   re -

leave   of your nymphs of   the   shore,   And   si - lence their mourn-ing With   vows of   re -

leave   of your nymphs of   the   shore,   And   si - lence their mourn-ing With   vows of   re -

turn‑ing, But never in‑tend‑ing to vis‑it them more, no nev‑er in‑tend‑ing to

turn‑ing, But nev‑er in‑tend‑ing to vis‑it them more, no nev‑er in‑tend‑ing to

turn‑ing, But nev‑er in‑tend‑ing to vis‑it them more, no nev‑er in‑tend‑ing to

turn‑ing, But nev‑er in‑tend‑ing to vis‑it them more, no nev‑er in‑tend‑ing to

Act III [*scene i*]

vis - it them more,   no ne-ver,   no nev-er,   in - tend - ing to_ vis - it them more!

vis - it them more,   no ne-ver,   no nev-er,   in - tend - ing to vis - it them more!

vis - it them more,   no ne-ver,   no nev-er,   in - tend - ing to   vis - it them more!

vis - it them more,   no ne-ver,   no nev-er,   in - tend - ing to vis - it them more!

f   *p*   *f*

30 The Sailors' Dance

ho— ho— ho! ho— ho— ho— ho— ho! E - lis - sa dies to - night, And

ho! ho— ho! E - lis - sa dies to - night, And

ho— ho— ho! ho— ho— ho— ho! E - lis - sa dies to - night, And

ho— ho! ho— ho! E - lis - sa dies to - night, And

Car-thage flames to - mor-row! De - night, And Car - thage flames to - mor - row!

Car-thage flames to - mor-row! De - night, And Car-thage flames to - mor - row!

Car-thage flames to - mor-row! De - night, And Car-thage flames to - mor - row!

Car-thage flames to - mor-row! De - night, And Car-thage flames to - mor - row!

34 The Witches' Dance -
{*Jack o' Lantern leads the Spaniards out of their way among the Inchanteresses*}

[SCENE II – *The Palace*]

heaven con-spire my fall. To Fate I sue, of o-ther means be-reft, The on - ly

re-fuge for the wretch - ed_ left.   See, ma-dam, see where the Prince ap-pears! Such

BELINDA   [Aeneas enters]

sor-row in his look he bears As would con-vince you still he's true. What   shall lost   Ae -

AENEAS

ne - as do?   How,   how, roy-al fair, shall I im-part The gods' de - cree,   and tell you

DIDO: we must part? Thus on the fa-tal banks of Nile Weeps the de-ceit-ful cro-co-dile; Thus hy-po-crites that mur-der act Make heav'n and gods the au-thors of the fact!

AENEAS: By all that's good... DIDO: By all that's good, no more! All that's good you have for-swore. To your pro-mis'd em-pire fly,— And let for-sa-ken Di-do die. AENEAS: In

Death, a - las!__ I can-not shun; Death must come when he is_gone.

36

Violin I

Violin II

Viola

CHORUS
SOPRANO

Great minds a - gainst them-selves con - spire, great minds, great minds a - gainst, a -

ALTO

Great minds a - gainst them-selves con - spire, great minds, great minds a - gainst, a -

TENOR

Great minds a - gainst them-selves con - spire, great minds, great minds a - gainst, a -

BASS

Great minds a - gainst them-selves con - spire, great minds, great minds a -

Sostenuto [♩ = ♩]

mf

for - get my — fate. Re - mem-ber me!   re - mem-ber me!   but

ah! _____ for-get   my   fate,   re - mem-ber me!   but   ah! _____

RITOR.

for - get my — fate.

MICHAEL TILMOUTH

A Newly-Composed Finale for the Grove Scene

To follow Aeneas's exit at "But with more ease could die",
p. 152, deriving in part from the brief prelude (no. 53) in
Act V of Purcell's *The Fairy-Queen*.

Michael Tilmouth, Tovey Professor of Music at the University of Edinburgh, is a
noted authority on seventeenth-century instrumental music. He is the current
president of the Purcell Society and has edited the trio sonatas for *The Works of
Henry Purcell*.

CRITICISM AND ANALYSIS

GEORGE BERNARD SHAW

[A Trip to Bow]†

The first staged revival of *Dido and Aeneas* in modern times was at the Royal College of Music in 1895, but the opera had been fairly well known to concert-goers for at least 100 years before that. On 21 February 1889, the editor of *The Star* asked his ace music critic George Bernard Shaw (alias Corno di Bassetto) to attend a concert performance of it in East London. Faced with the prospect of a dreary journey to regions unknown, Shaw demurred. But when he learned that "Purcell! the greatest of English composers" would be left to the mercy of a rival critic ("a man whose abnormal gifts in every other direction have blinded him to his utter ignorance of music"), he snatched the tickets from the editor's desk, armed himself with a revolver, and set off for Bow.

* * * When I got into the concert room I was perfectly dazzled by the appearance of the orchestra. Nearly all the desks for the second violins were occupied by ladies: beautiful young ladies. Personal beauty is not the strong point of West End orchestras, and I thought the change an immense improvement until the performance began, when the fair fiddlers rambled from bar to bar with a certain sweet indecision that had a charm of its own, but was not exactly what Purcell and Handel meant. When I say that the performance began, I do not imply that it began punctually. The musicians began to drop in at about ten minutes past eight, and the audience were inclined to remonstrate; but an occasional apology from the conductor, Mr. F.A.W. Docker, kept them in good humor.

Dido and Eneas is 200 years old, and not a bit the worse for wear. I daresay many of the Bowegians thought that the unintentional quaintnesses of the amateurs in the orchestra were Purcellian antiquities. If so, they were never

† From *Shaw's Music: the Complete Musical Criticism in Three Volumes*, ed. Dan H. Laurence (London: Bodley Head, 1981), I, 559–560. Reprinted by permission of The Society of Authors on behalf of the Bernard Shaw Estate.

more mistaken in their lives. Henry Purcell was a great composer: a very great composer indeed; and even this little boarding-school opera is full of his spirit, his freshness, his dramatic expression, and his unapproached art of setting English speech to music. The Handel Society did not do him full justice: the work, in fact, is by no means easy; but the choir made up bravely for the distracting dances of the string quartet. Eneas should not have called Dido Deedo, any more than Juliet should call Romeo Ro-*may*-oh, or Othello call his wife Days-*day*-mona. If Purcell chose to pronounce Dido English fashion, it is not for a Bow-Bromley tenor to presume to correct him. Belinda, too, was careless in the matter of time. She not only arrived after her part had been half finished by volunteers from the choir, but in Oft She Visits she lost her place somewhat conspicuously. An unnamed singer took Come away, fellow sailors, come away: that salt sea air that makes you wonder how anyone has ever had the face to compose another sailor's song after it. I quote the concluding lines, and wish I could quote the incomparably jolly and humorous setting: —

Take a bowsy short leave of your nymphs on the shore;
   And silence their mourning
   With vows of returning,
Though never intending to visit them more.

SAILORS *(greatly tickled)*. Though never—!
OTHER SAILORS *(ready to burst with laughter)*. Though never—!
ALL *(uproariously)*. Inte-en-ding to vi-sit them more.

I am sorry to have to add that the Handel choir, feeling that they were nothing if not solemn, contrived to subdue this rousing strain to the decorum of a Sunday school hymn; and it missed fire accordingly. * * *

ANDREW PORTER

[British Worthy]†

Andrew Porter has done as much to improve the quality of music criticism in the present age as Shaw did in his. An organ scholar at Oxford where he also read English, Porter edited *The Musical Times* from 1960 to 1967, emigrating to the United States in 1972 to become the music critic of *The New Yorker*. His criticism is distinguished by an unapologetic inclusion of textual and contextual issues surrounding the work and performance at hand. A vigorous and compelling advocate of Italian *opera seria*, particularly Handel's, Porter also champions Purcell's stage works with a true Shavian spirit.

Purcell's *Dido and Aeneas* has not lacked praise, but I don't think it has been praised enough. Jack Westrup, in the Master Musicians volume on the composer, calls it "a masterpiece, but not, as is sometimes claimed, a flawless masterpiece."[1] Robert Etheridge Moore, in *Henry Purcell and the Restoration Theatre*, calls it a "dramatic masterpiece" and yet not "by any means a flawless work."[2] Joseph Kerman, in *Opera as Drama*, speaks of its "dramatic perfection"[3] but finds the recitative "impersonal, courtly, and bombastic."[4] All three commentators suggest that the expression of Aeneas' agony on receiving the apparently divine command to leave Carthage, desert Dido, and found Rome is somewhat perfunctory. And I, who sometimes think that *Dido and Aeneas* is just about the only flawless opera — well, remembering *Cosi fan tutte*, perhaps I should say the only flawless operatic tragedy — ever written, would claim that Aeneas's soliloquy at the end of Act II is a perfectly proportioned piece of composition, exactly what is called for at this crisis in the drama. The harmonies are wrested as violently as the hero's heart; his E-major cry of "Yours be the blame, ye Gods, for I obey your will" sounds an ironic echo of his boast in Act I that he will "defie the Feeble stroke of Destiny." Here Aeneas, in Acts I and III a suppliant, comes into his own. The outer acts belong to Dido, but in Act II she sings only a single couplet. The

† From *Music of Three More Seasons 1977–1980* (New York: Alfred A. Knopf, 1981), pp. 355–6. Copyright © 1981 by Andrew Porter. Reprinted by permission.

1. [See below, p. 202]
2. [See below, p. 220]
3. [See below, p. 224]
4. [See below, p. 227]

words ("The Skies are Clouded") are ominous; the harmony, decorated fanfares of D major, points to the G minor of her final entrance and lament; the figuration adumbrates the violent phrases in which she is to dismiss Aeneas.

Nahum Tate's libretto has come in for its share of scorn. His seven-line stanza for Dido's lament, it's been said, doesn't scan:

> *Thy Hand,* Belinda, *darkness shades me,*
> *On thy Bosom let me rest,*
> *More I wou'd but Death invades me.*
> *Death is now a Welcom Guest.*
> *When I am laid in Earth* [*may*] *my wrongs Create*
> *No trouble in thy Breast,*
> *Remember me, but ah! forget my Fate.*

These are verses of a kind that Dryden, in the preface to *his* libretto for Purcell, *King Arthur, or The British Worthy*, described as "rugged to the Reader, that they may be harmonious to the Hearer." He knew that "the Numbers of Poetry and Vocal Musick . . . are sometimes contrary." And Tate plainly knew it, too. Purcell sets Tate's first four lines in recitative; the skillful construction of the last three (Purcell added the *may*) allows him to expand them into that great lament declaimed in spans of four, five, six, or seven bars over a regular five-bar ground bass. Dido's first air has a five-line stanza:

> *Ah!* Belinda, *I am prest*
> *With Torment not to be confest.*
> *Peace and I are Strangers grown.*
> *I Languish till my Grief is known,*
> *Yet wou'd not have it Guest.*

Here Purcell sets the first two lines as arioso, the last three as an air in periods of four, five, or six bars; and he binds arioso and air together by placing both of them over a four-bar ground bass. In both the air and the lament, the vocal and the ground-bass cadences seldom coincide: the repeated bass treads on inexorably, while the song flows and surges with the heroine's thoughts, falls silent for a moment, rings out again, repeats words with a new, fierce intensity. In both pieces, when the singer is done — in Westrup's words, "when the heart is so charged that there is nothing more to add" — the strings alone take over the burden. Neither piece comes to a full close but flows on into the next number. Tate's libretto seems to me at once settable, subtle, and beautiful. The Trojan sailors' lusty, insouciant farewell to their Carthaginian lasses forms a potent prelude to and commentary on Aeneas' desertion of Dido. Less obviously, the epithalamic wish so brightly sung near the start of the opera, "*Cupids* Strew your path with Flowers," finds its tragic fulfillment in the final chorus:

With drooping Wings you Cupids come,
To scatter Roses on her Tomb.

Purcell must have known both Lully's and Carissimi's music. He commanded both the French and the Italian manners, and to them he added a mastery of English declamation which has never been excelled. He discovered for himself operatic secrets known to Monteverdi: the balance of free declamation and formal structure, the matching of dissonance and resolution to emotional tension and release, a control of dramatic tempo—knowing when to bate, when to press on—and a feeling for melodic contour and vocal register that make inner emotion explicit. Moreover, he and Tate anticipated what Gluck and Calzabigi, seventy years later, were to strive for in *Orfeo*: directness of dramatic expression, an absence of frills, the presentation of a coherent drama that moves swiftly—but variously, through scenes of changing emotion—to its tragic close, and a protagonist who, with dignity and passion, sings from the heart to touch the hearts of all who listen. * * *

JACK WESTRUP

[*A Flawed Masterpiece*]†

Sir Jack Westrup (1904–1975), Heather Professor of Music at Oxford from 1947 to 1971, was a great debunker of pretentious and chauvinistic writings on music. His 1937 Master Musicians book on Purcell, from which the following extract is taken, is a classic in the life-and-works genre. Purged of all anecdote and gushing admiration, it removed Purcell from a Victorian plaster-of-Paris pedestal and placed him on one of granite. Westrup's sometimes harsh criticisms of *Dido and Aeneas* were intended to shock complacent readers, but they also reveal the source of the opera's greatness.

* * * As a poet [Tate] deserves all the unkind things that have been said about him, but whatever the literary quality of *Dido*—and it is on the whole very poor—there is no doubt that the text is thoroughly suitable for musical

† From *Purcell*, rev. Nigel Fortune (London: J. M. Dent, 1980), pp. 115–125. Reprinted with permission.

setting. There is little of Dryden's anxious preoccupation with feminine end-ings or literary graces. The style is plain and straightforward, with only one or two deviations into theatrical pomposity, and the words are such as any musi-cian would welcome. One has only to think of occasional lines — 'Peace and I are strangers grown,' 'Fear no danger to ensue,' 'Great minds against them-selves conspire,' and so on — to see what opportunities lay ready to Purcell's hand. And how magnificently he seized those opportunities!

The story in its essentials is Vergil's. Aeneas, fleeing from ruined Troy and bound for Latium, is driven by storm into Carthage, where the widowed Dido reigns as queen. Proximity leads to passion, felt and reciprocated; but the gods forbid their union. Aeneas sails away to fulfil his destiny in Italy and Dido ends her sorrows with her own hand. To this simple story the poet has merely added the witches, as symbols of the malevolence of destiny, and modified the tragic ending by making Dido the victim of a broken heart.[1] The work begins with a short overture of the type established by Lulli — a slow intro-duction followed by a quasi-fugal *allegro*. Thereafter we are plunged straight into the anguish of love. Belinda, Dido's sister — corresponding to Anna in Vergil — plays the part of the confidante, a type familiar in seventeenth-century Italian opera and well exemplified by Arnalta in Monteverdi's *Incoronazione di Poppea*. She counsels cheerfulness and the chorus echo her advice, but in vain. Dido's pangs are beyond remedy. She confesses them in an aria that at once illustrates Purcell's gifts both of musical invention and of dramatic char-acterization. The movement is constructed on a simple ground bass of four bars, above which the queen's sighs are heard:

1. This seems to be implied by the final recitative. There is certainly nothing in the text to suggest suicide, unless we interpret literally the words 'Elissa bleeds to-night.'

As the song proceeds the bass becomes more insistent. It has been the background to the voice. Now it invades the singer's consciousness and its opening phrase shapes itself to her words:

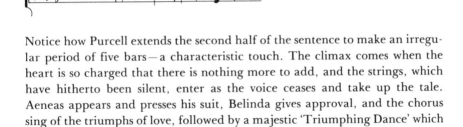

Notice how Purcell extends the second half of the sentence to make an irregular period of five bars — a characteristic touch. The climax comes when the heart is so charged that there is nothing more to add, and the strings, which have hitherto been silent, enter as the voice ceases and take up the tale. Aeneas appears and presses his suit, Belinda gives approval, and the chorus sing of the triumphs of love, followed by a majestic 'Triumphing Dance' which recalls the stately chaconne — also in C major — in Lulli's *Cadmus et Hermione*.

Scene ii* brings us to the Sorceress's cave. The chorus are now witches, singing 'Ho ho ho' as energetically and in the same tempo as the three magicians in Lulli's *comédie-ballet, Pastorale comique* — or we may compare the shattering 'Tôt tôt tôt' of the chorus of Chalybes, forging steel, in the same composer's *Isis*. Here we cannot help being struck by the unreality of Restoration conventions. Purcell's instrumental introduction is solemn and impressive but it does not suggest the horror of the supernatural, and the choruses are jolly rather than frightening. The witches may sing, 'Harm's our delight and mischief all our skill,' but they might just as well be a crowd of rustic merrymakers for all the music does to help illusion. The one really striking moment is the suggestion of distant hunting-horns on the strings when the Sorceress refers to the joint expedition. * * *

*[Act II, scene i, in the present edition.]

Act II [scene ii] introduces the hunting-party. It includes the stately aria in which an attendant woman recites the melancholy fate of Actaeon, the voice pursuing its own richly varied course above one of those steadily moving basses in which the seventeenth century delighted. Once again the entry of the strings at the end supplies the culminating passion. The storm follows. Belinda, brisk and practical as ever, urges the company to return to the city in a lively little song that exactly hits off her nurse-like anxiety. The chorus dutifully repeat her advice. Aeneas, confronted by a spirit in the guise of Mercury, learns that he must leave Carthage that very night. The scene ends with his anguished realization of the sacrifice that obedience entails.

The atmosphere changes completely in Act III. We are on the quay-side with the rough, homely members of Aeneas's crew, who have received their sailing orders and are already preparing departure. The stir and bustle are vividly expressed in the orchestral introduction:

It will help us to appreciate Purcell's relationship to his contemporaries and predecessors if we compare with this two other instrumental pieces, the first from Blow's *Venus and Adonis* and the second from the introductory symphony to Marc'Antonio Ziani's opera, *La schiava fortunata* (an adaptation of Cesti's *La Semirami*)[2]:

2. Quoted by A. Heuss, 'Die venetianischen Opern-Sinfonien,' *Sammelbände der Internationalen Musikgesellschaft*, iv, 1902–3.

The climax of Purcell's symphony is one of those swinging, inevitable tunes of which he seemed to hold the peculiar secret. It is a perfect match for Tate's racy jingle:

> Come away, fellow sailors, come away,
>> Your anchors be weighing,
>> Time and tide will admit no delaying;
> Take a boozy short leave of your nymphs on the shore,
>> And silence their mourning
>> With vows of returning,
> But never intending to visit them more,
> No, never intending to visit them more,

with a Scotch snap for the jaunty repetition, 'No, never.' When next we hear the chorus, after solos by the Sorceress and her henchwomen, they are witches, singing 'Destruction's our delight' in square-cut, four-part harmony, with little bits of imitation for the wicked 'Ho hos.' The style of this is similar to Lulli's sturdy homophonic choruses or those of the Venetian composers. Its origin is to be found in the popular part-songs of Renaissance Italy, with their imitative 'fa la las,' which had been domesticated in England by Thomas Morley before the end of the sixteenth century.

The time has come for farewell, and farewell is bound to be not only sad but stormy. Stung by Dido's reproaches, Aeneas for a moment threatens to disobey Jupiter's decree. But the queen is ready to meet her fate and will hear of no weakening. With her heart breaking she sends him imperiously away. There follows one of the most impressive moments in the opera, when the chorus, fulfilling the function of its Greek prototype, comments gravely on the strange contradiction of human passions:

> Great minds against themselves conspire,
> And shun the cure they most desire.

The words sound perfunctory, but Purcell has set them to a solemn, chorale-like measure that rises to the proper height of tragic dignity. It leads straight into the final lament. With none but the faithful Belinda by her side, the queen, deserted and already in the shadows, sings her own threnody:

> Thy hand, Belinda, darkness shades me,
> On thy bosom let me rest;
> More I would, but death invades me,
> Death is now a welcome guest.
> When I am laid in earth, may my wrongs create
> No trouble in thy breast;
> Remember me, but ah! forget my fate.

It has been said that the words will not scan, but that is not strictly true. The fifth line is clumsy and lop-sided, but it can just be fitted into a metrical scheme. Even so the verse remains a bungling piece of work. All the more remarkable then is the way in which Purcell has treated it. Of the first four lines he makes a pathetic recitative, and reserves the last three for one of his noblest lyrical inspirations, in which technique and passion are miraculously fused in one. It is constructed upon a ground bass, one of the favourite devices of the age and widely used for laments in Italian operas. 'The practice,' says Burney, 'was Gothic'[3] and damns it by implication, though he admits that some composers were successful in adopting it. The judgment is unsound, since no musical device is necessarily bad in itself. Undoubtedly the ground bass was a mine that Purcell in particular was apt to overwork; but here he struck a vein of purest gold:

---

3. *A General History of Music* (1776–89), III, 494.

The commonest type of ground bass used by the Italians was the descending scale, either diatonic or chromatic. Purcell here uses the latter, adding a cadence to complete it. The challenge of such a bass to a composer's invention is obvious. It is not enough in so pathetic an aria to supply a graceful melodic line and fill up the interval with conventional figured harmony. The successful treatment of a ground bass of this type depends on the skilful use of suspensions and discords. Purcell seizes on this opportunity in the second bar of the voice part, where the B flat is a suspension or 'hang-over' from the previous bar. The result is what is technically known as an appoggiatura in the second bar, a device that has been for several hundred years a peculiar vehicle for emotional expression in music. How close Purcell's kinship is to the Italian composers can be seen by examining the following extract from a lament in Cavalli's *Egisto* (1643):

Here too we have the descending chromatic scale and the appoggiaturas, both of which Bach later used with such striking effect in the 'Crucifixus' of his Mass in B minor.

In Purcell's song the accompaniment is not for continuo alone but for strings. Nothing is left to chance and every detail of the harmony is preserved intact. When the voice turns from a flowing melody to the monotoned appeal, 'Remember me,' the violins take over the appoggiaturas and continue them to the end. In the last nine bars the orchestra alone sets the seal on the lamentation:

Handel may have had this passage in mind when he wrote the chorus 'How long, O Lord, shall Israel groan?' in *Susanna*, which is also over a chromatically descending ground bass. Purcell himself used the bass again in the introduction to the duet, 'In vain the am'rous flute,' in the 1692 *Ode on St. Cecilia's Day*, but not as a ground. What has once been worked perfectly is best left alone.

Dido's lament has justly come to be regarded as one of the great things in music. Here Purcell rises within narrow limits to monumental grandeur. The brief aria has a Miltonic dignity; in that last repeated 'Remember me' it is almost as though the musician, tearing himself away from the artificiality of court and theatre, had written his own epitaph. It is succeeded by a little chorus that rounds off the work with the same tragic finality as the last chorus in the St. Matthew Passion. And having sung it once the chorus must sing it again so that the drooping cadences may linger in the memory.

Dido is a masterpiece, but not, as is sometimes claimed, a flawless masterpiece. Purcell was thirty when he wrote it, but he had had very little experience of the stage; and indeed the limited scope of the work would try the gifts even of a musician who had spent long years in contact with the theatre. The work is sometimes praised because it moves swiftly; but that is not necessarily a virtue in opera. Opera, like the spoken drama, can afford to linger over moments, to extend and elaborate an emotional crisis until the spectator is himself willy-nilly caught and enfolded in the passions of the persons on the stage. It is impossible not to feel in *Dido* that the episodes and individual movements sometimes succeed each other too rapidly. We learn of Dido's passion in two exquisitely expressive arias, but of Aeneas's we hear no more than a few bars of recitative. When the two lovers sing together at the end it is merely to fling protests at each other, and the treatment is conventional. Conventional too is the duet of the two witches in the last act, where the ready-made sequences of Italian opera take the place of real horror. Indeed, Purcell is at his weakest in dealing with the witches. It is the human beings in this opera that have inspired him to his greatest heights. It has been said that Dido 'is more than half a schoolgirl herself, with a court of schoolgirls round her,'[4] but that is not quite true. There is nothing callow in Purcell's Dido. She is from first to last a tragic heroine. Dent pointed out that German critics have described the work as 'Shakespearian,'[5] and it is easy to realize the justice of the epithet.

I have ventured on these criticisms of the structure of *Dido*, since it has become almost an article of faith with some Purcellians to accept the work as faultless. The truth is that no composer could adequately treat such a tremendous subject in what is, in effect, a one-act opera. What makes *Dido* immortal is that it triumphs over its weaknesses. It will always hold our admiration and affection for its penetrating revelation of the profoundest secrets of human passion. Standing midway between the English masque and the Italian cantata it was the prelude to an achievement that was never realized, either by Purcell or by his successors. When Italian opera came to London in the eighteenth century, recitative had become mainly a conventional thread for linking together a succession of arias. Purcell's recitative, which clearly owes something to Locke, is faithful to the older model; it is a brilliant application of the declamatory style to the peculiar accents of English verse. It has nothing of the ambling fluency of Lulli's recitative. It is direct and forceful and moves constantly within the limits of common time. The conventions of chromatic progression and falling intervals—perfect and diminished fifths, perfect and diminished fourths—are used, but with an appropriateness that justifies every one of them. Only the florid clichés that have to do duty for storm and stress seem forced and unnatural. * * *

---

4. H. C. Colles, *Voice and Verse: A Study in English Song* (London, 1928), p. 85.
5. *Foundations of English Opera*; see below, p. 214.

WILFIRD MELLERS

The Tragic Heroine and the Un-Hero†

Wilfrid Mellers's analysis of *Dido and Aeneas* places the opera against the background of seventeenth-century English heroic drama, which, in spite of repeated
and extravagant attempts to be tragic, was unable to achieve the level of intensity that Purcell and Tate reached as if by accident. Mellers's writings on music
span the gamut from François Couperin to Bob Dylan, and nearly all of them,
including the following essay, discuss the fusion of words and music as a social,
not merely an artistic, phenomenon.

In Louis XIV's France, heroic opera was closely associated with heroic tragedy; in early seventeenth-century England our failure to produce the one was
consequent on our failure to produce the other. In his two tragedies Ben
Jonson had attempted the heroic, seeking an art "high and aloof," involving
"truth of argument, dignity of persons, gravity and height of elocution, ful-
ness and frequency of sentence." But *Sejanus* and *Catiline* had little success
and no successors; and theatrical enterprise was disrupted by the Civil War
and during the Protectorate. After the Restoration * * * values had changed.
The new society was middle-class and mercantile; and though it had grandi-
ose ambitions, it had no grandeur of spirit. Both the moral core and the sense
of stylization were lacking, and when dramatists attempted the heroic, it was
from disillusioned wishful-thinking, rather than from conviction. If we are
not in truth heroic, we can put up a show of heroism: so the Tragic Hero will
evoke admiration, not compassion. Even the conflict between Love and Duty
was less important than the display of simulated emotion it could give rise to.
From this point of view Restoration tragedy was essentially a public art,
meaningless apart from its audience. * * * The dramatic and literary styliza-

† Reprinted with slight modifications from *Harmonious Meeting: A Study of the Relationships between English Music, Poetry and Theatre, c. 1600–1900* (London: Dennis Dobson, 1965),
pp. 203–14, by permission of the author.

tions—the multiplicity of "crises," the heightened diction, the paradoxes, antitheses, rhetorical questions and other devices—existed to exaggerate the display, not (as in Racine) to control the intensity of feeling in the interests of civilization. Restoration comedy is also nothing if not a public act in so far as it is not, like Molière's comedy (which the English dramatists emulated), a comedy of manners and morals, but of manners only, and mostly bad manners at that. We are invited to admire Millament and Mirabelle for the face they present to the world. Indeed, they illustrate "the way of the world" because they function effectively in it—without being taken in *by* it. A comedy of simulated feeling may be tolerable because there is inevitably an element of disillusion in the comic approach; a tragedy of simulation is, however, a contradiction in terms.

The book of *Dido and Aeneas* was a rewriting, for music, of a full-scale heroic tragedy by Nahum Tate, called *Brutus of Alba*. The idea of translating it into an opera book was probably prompted by Blow's *Venus and Adonis*; but whereas Blow's work was conceived as a court masque and turned into an opera almost fortuitously, *Dido* was conceived as a drama which, in being transformed into an opera, became more, not less, dramatic. In part the improvement was technical. Since Restoration tragedy is an art of inflation, almost any example of the genre would be improved by having the words reduced by two-thirds, as was necessary if the piece was to be sung—especially at the end of term school concert. (We can afford to sacrifice the kind of language in which Brutus-Aeneas decides to leave the Queen:

> Give notice to the Fleet we sail to Night.
> Said I to Night! Forsake the Queen to Night!
> Forsake! oh Fate! the Queen! to Night forsake her!)

None the less, there was more involved than a technical improvement; for although the opera still accepts the traditional heroic theme, it subtly modifies it in the light of contemporary English experience. The masque opposition of love-destruction, order-disorder, is still present in Tate's libretto; but private and public order no longer become synonymous in an act of homage to Hymen. Although there is conflict between love and duty, the two forces are no longer equally weighted. In Tate's middle-classical world, public duty becomes the destructive force; and the only reality is now personal experience—Dido's love for Aeneas. From this point of view Tate makes a significant modification to the classical myth. In Virgil's story Aeneas is called back to duty by the gods. In Tate's libretto he is called away by a witch *masquerading* as a god. This is indeed the ultimate inversion: for the antimasque witches now "stand for" the values of the masque. Thus it is dramatically important that Aeneas should appear a poor thing. The point is that he prefers to accept a sham (conventional) duty rather than reality (or love).[1]

This duality is already present in the overture. The slow opening section takes us immediately into the world of Dido's suffering: the stabbing dissonant suspensions, the lamenting chromatics, anticipate her arioso though they are ennobled, depersonalized, by the sustained lyricism, the grave movement, the pedal notes. The quick section, in sprightly quavers, is dance music, as we would expect. But it is not the conventional, triple-rhythmed round: and is curiously unimposing if it is supposed to represent public glory. Indeed, it sounds suspiciously like the witches' music: and prepares us for the identification of opposites that is to come later.

The action opens with Belinda and the chorus, both representing public or social values, trying to cheer Dido up. Belinda sings in dance movement, of course; in the jaunty Restoration dotted rhythm that was a cruder version of the *notes inégales* in French ceremonial music. "Shake the cloud from off your brow," she says. After all, Empire's growing, pleasures are flowing, fortune smiles and so should you; we can enjoy the best of every world, with public glory and personal satisfaction working together. The minor key, the slightly dissonant texture of the choral parts, the physical action in Belinda's ornamentation intimate, perhaps, that life isn't as easy as all that. Anyway, when the chorus is interrupted by the lamenting Dido we know at once that hers is a deeper and richer reality. She creates herself before our eyes and ears —like Blow's Venus in Act III, or Purcell's Blessed Virgin. Her arioso line,

---

1. Some commentators take the view that Aeneas is given a "poor" part, with no arias, for practical reasons: he would have to be played by a man, smuggled into a girls' school! It might more convincingly be argued that Tate and Purcell and Josias Priest, having taken the trouble to smuggle him, would have made as much use of him as possible; in any case Purcell, like all great creative intelligences, was adept at turning practical necessity to artistic purpose.

What he could not deal with was the artistic convention that no longer had human significance. Tate's libretto included a prologue in the manner of the pastoral masque, celebrating Phoebus and Venus ("Her charms bless the Night, as his Beams bless the Day . . . She gives our Flocks their feeding, He makes 'em fit for Breeding"): a conventional tribute to the Golden Age we live in, though the tone is low. Purcell wouldn't have objected to the tone; but it seems probable that he did object to the content, since the celebrative masque was extraneous to a work that is, in a philosophical, not technical sense, an *anti*-masque. In any case, no music for this prologue survives. Some authorities think Purcell wrote it, because the opera is so short without it. But the addition of the masque would hardly make the piece into an evening's entertainment; and a one-hour piece seems adequate if, as was probable, it was combined with other school activities. No explanation has been proffered as to why the masque music should have been lost while the opera survives [but see above, Price, pp. 18–19]. Another, more recent, theory is that Daniel Purcell wrote the masque music for a revival. See the essay by Eric Walter White, "New Light on *Dido and Aeneas*," *Henry Purcell 1659–1695*, ed. Imogen Holst (Oxford, 1959), pp. 14–34. [Compare the argument in favor of John Eccles, above, Price, p. 17.]

broken in rhythm by her sighs, tense with Lombard sobs, weeping appoggia-turas and languishing chromatics, creates within us the "torment that cannot be confess'd" so that we enter, momentarily, into her being. At the same time, her emotional arioso is poised over a ground bass, so that it remotely presages her final lament. When she takes over the ground theme and sings it in canon with the bass, to the words "Peace and I are strangers grown," she is at once a suffering woman and a queen. The "ceremonial" chaconne succours personal distress; we already know that Dido is the true tragic heroine, because she will suffer all, sacrifice all, for the integrity of her love.

Belinda, still belonging to the practical world, then suggests that Dido is getting worked up gratuitously. Why shouldn't she tell her love? Why shouldn't she and Aeneas marry and live happily ever after? Private love need not neces-sarily be in conflict with public duty; on the contrary, monarchs *uniting* ought to create order and peace. This is taken up by the chorus in rigid, rather insensitive dance homophony. Dido cuts them short, however, and breaks into still more impassioned arioso. She vividly invokes Aeneas both in his public, war-like valor (trumpet figurations) and in potential amatory bliss (softly caressing suspensions). This time her passion finds no resolution in aria: we begin to suspect that she is so upset because the realities of love are so disturbing (her shooting scales on the words "What storms" significantly anticipate the storm which the witches will unleash). She knows, like any classical heroine, that you cannot have both Honor and Love at the same time: but not so much because (like a classical heroine) she believes in Honor as because she doubts whether Aeneas's love is as honest as hers. Belinda is so moved that she turns from the social world and, sympathizing with Dido, sings her mistress's kind of arioso.

But Belinda perhaps regards this as weakness: for she turns abruptly back to her social role and, in duet with an anonymous Woman, representa-tive of Society, sings the jaunty "Fear no danger to ensue." Don't worry, they say with the infuriating helpfulness of the unimaginative, it may never hap-pen; we're *sure* the hero loves as well as you do. We return, of course, to bouncy, self-confident dance meter, reinforced by the syncopated rhythm and the perpetual parallel thirds. The deliberate unreality of this is suggested by the first appearance of the major key and perhaps by the perky rhythm which makes hay of the verbal accents. In arioso Purcell's accentuation is always meticulous, growing inevitably from the way in which the character would speak in passion. Here, if the false accents are not deliberate, they are the kind of accident that happens only to genius. They make the "*ever* gentle *ever* smiling" hero seem slightly fatuous. There is the briefest hint of minor tonality when the chorus invites Cupids to strew the lovers' path with flowers.

This is a most delicate piece of irony: for when Cupids do in fact strew flowers at the end they do so on Dido's dead body, in an elegy on the care-free careless paradise that Belinda, the Woman, and the Chorus sing of in this dance-song.

Ironically too, Aeneas appears immediately on the conclusion of the fatuous ditty. Belinda—a public figure—describes him as god-like. But his first arioso, though serious enough, contains a hint of melodrama, of rhetorical self-dramatization, especially in the descending diminished seventh on the words "no fate but you." (The interval is common in Handel, of course, but sufficiently rare in the music of Purcell's time to call attention to itself.) There may also be a suggestion of self-indulgence in the tritonal arabesque he sings on the word "feeble."

The love match is symbolized, as Cupid "throws the dart that's dreadful," in a bit of traditional counterpoint—a canon two in one (!) that creates, within its unity and its regular dance meter, a rather painfully dissonant texture. Aeneas's famous remark "If not for mine, for Empire's sake, Some pity on your lover take" puts the situation pretty accurately so far as he is concerned. The material benefits of the match, he hints, are not to be sniffed at; how would it look to the World if she were to turn down a Hero! So it is appropriate that Belinda should follow with a deliberately conventional pursuit aria that deflates the love-experience of the truth Dido has put into it. Belinda's song is in the major, of course: a love-chase with virtually no dissonance, and with "echoes" between voice and bass, to suggest illusion. The echoes, here, are a part of the game; but when the chorus rounds off the scene with a ceremonial dance-chorus in triple rhythm, with lilting dotted movement, the echoes (on the significant words "cool shady fountains") bring in a sudden, disturbing modulation to the minor of the dominant, followed by a false relation. So here they hint at illusion in another and deeper sense, highly characteristic of seventeenth-century echoes: at the *other* reality, the world beyond this ostensible material triumph. Perhaps this is why the final triumph dance, though still in the major, has become a little uneasy, with sharply accented dissonant passing notes that hint that all may not, after all, be for the best in the best of all possible worlds.

In any case we move from the Triumph directly to the second scene—and the Witches' Cave.[2] The Sorceress was Nahum Tate's invention, and is a

---

2. Tate's libretto concludes Act I with the Triumphing Dance, making the Sorceress scene the beginning of Act II. This would seem to be the proper place for the act division and perhaps only practical problems of stage mechanics prompted a modification. On the other hand it might be argued that the shock effect of the contrast between public triumph and the horror within would be weakened if there were a break before the Sorceress's appearance, and that the unreality of the hunting idyll is stressed if it is, as it were, self-enclosed.

fundamentally serious creation. Her music—in the sub-dominant minor, the traditional key for *chants lugubres*—contains excruciating suspended minor seconds, angular leaps and chromaticisms; yet it is spacious and noble, in the same style as the opening of the overture, and is directly comparable with Dido's arioso in both intensity and span. On no account should the Sorceress be treated grotesquely. She must have a Circe-like grandeur, because the destructive force is a reality, like love. Both, indeed, are within Dido, which is why she is a tragic character. Few people are capable of "real" experience, true love. Rather than face up to the creative *and* destructive principles within us, we prefer to substitute something easier, such as Aeneas's "Empire."

Whereas Belinda had justly pointed out that the fulfillment of private love might lead to public prosperity, the Sorceress announces—in an exact inversion of heroic convention—that she intends to destroy Dido as an individual and at the same time bring ruin to the State through the anarchy of War. Moreover, she will do this by means of an assertion of public duty! From the standpoint of convention, her attitude will be absolutely "correct." This is why her rout of witches sing music that is identical in style with the ceremonial dance choruses except that it is quicker, more perfunctory. The anti-masque is now on the side of order, because order is presented as destructive of human integrity. The relationship of the witches to the Sorceress is similar to the relationship of his rout to Comus. Unlike the Sorceress they are funny: their quick music is based on the kind of music Lully composed for his *comic* operas and ballets. None the less they are also horrid, because incapable of apprehending the realities of passion. In a way they are naturalistic and contemporary: not so much supernatural as a gang of middle-class female gossips and harridans whose mentality is neatly characterized in their notorious couplet: "Our plot has took, the Queen's forsook." Their ha-ha-ha's are horrifying only because they are grossly inane.

The witches do not always depart so radically from heroic convention. Sometimes they sing straight ceremonial music, like a masque chorus, the irony being in the situation, not the music. Two witches invoke the storm in a canon two in one, there being a kind of blasphemy in this destructive use of "doctrinal" counterpoint. There is certainly a blasphemy in the echo chorus "In our deep vaulted cell," the blasphemy being inherent in the singing of such nobly ceremonial masque-music by such low types. The echoes split up the words, literally destroy meaning: so this time the seventeenth-century echoes are illusion in a discreditable sense. The masque chorus is followed by another echo piece, a dance of furies, in which the texture is riddled with *false* relations and the echoes are a deceit. This illusory quality is the more pointed because the Sorceress's dark F minor has changed to a pastoral F major. Moreover, the echo-ritual and dance of furies are most cunningly placed. They immediately precede the idyll wherein Dido and Aeneas consummate their love: and so hint at the element of illusion within the idyll itself.

Act II [scene ii, the hunt], takes place away from the public world. As Belinda says, it is only "thanks to these lonesome vales" that Dido and Aeneas can be brought together. Belinda sings with a chorus of attendants in D minor, a key that is related to the pastoral dream of F major, but "real" because their love, or at least Dido's love, is real. The chorus sings a "pursuit" canon; but in gentle valedictory lyricism, with a number of sighing dissonances. An anonymous woman sings an aria on a ground bass which, recounting the Actaeon myth, offers an objective commentary on the human situation, suggesting how Dido's experience parallels the Actaeon story, since she is harried to death by the force of her own passion, as he was killed by his own hounds. Despite the level, impersonal movement of the bass, the aria grows more impassioned in melodic contour, rising to its climax on a high F sharp and G. Then the vocal line stops and the instrumental ritornello takes over, once more distancing the emotion as the attendants perform a graceful, ritualized dance. This extra-personal aria on a ground bass occurs halfway through the opera; it looks backwards to her first words, forwards to her last—both of which are arias over a ground.

This moment outside Time is interrupted by the storm, which the lovers regard as a perturbation of Nature, and so it is. But we know it is within their love, and an instrument of fate. The pastoral idyll, "the open field," is indeed "no shelter from this storm." Belinda and the chorus switch us brusquely back to the everyday world with the rising arpeggios of "Haste, haste to town."[3] Significantly, they go back to town, not to the heroic world of the court. Though the music is superficially agitated, it is jaunty, without interior dissonance, as unthinking and unfeeling as Belinda's earlier "pursuit" aria which, indeed, it reverses.

When they have gone cosily "out of the storm," the [elf of the] Sorceress appears, disguised as the god Mercury, and delivers the fateful message to Aeneas. His slithering "ah's" on hearing this are very different in effect from Dido's heartrent ululations. The first thing he thinks of is "what language can I try / My injured Queen to pacify?" A deflated hero indeed, he not only gives in to a God, which is what a real Hero ought to do after a struggle, but he gives in to a god that is a fake, and the first emotion he feels is fear of what

3. In Tate's libretto these words are most inappropriately given to Dido, who is a tragic figure precisely because she is incapable of running away from any storm. Perhaps this was merely a typographical error, which composer and librettist corrected when the text was musicked.

Dido may think, feel, maybe do. Yet there is an element of pathos in his position as unheroic hero. This comes out in his final pushing of the blame on to someone else ("*Yours*" — high E — "be the blame, ye gods"); in his submission (chord of the augmented fifth); and in his expressed preference for death, which he significantly thinks might be *easier* than facing Dido (declining phrases, broken by silences, but without much dissonance). We are meant to find this moving (Aeneas isn't the only weak man among us!) yet at the same time, as an end to the act, bathetic. And it isn't Aeneas who dies, but Dido.[4]

The last act opens with a different kind of reference to the World. This time it is Low, not High Life, perhaps because the witches have revealed to us that the values of high life are really low, or not values at all. Though we begin with a triple-rhythmed dance, in rudimentary fugato, it is not ceremonial, but a sailors' dance, brisk, popular in idiom. The song the sailor sings is again an ironic commentary on the sublime. All the sailors, he says, will be taking a "boozy short leave of their nymphs on the shore"; and the classical allusion to nymphs is a euphuism if ever there was one. Of course, all the sailors will give "vows of returning to silence their mourning" (mock chromatics descend through the dance lilt) but they know, and the nymphs know, they'll not be intending to visit them more. They couldn't, as we say today, care less, and when you come down to brass tacks their situation is just the same as that of Dido and Aeneas; so why all the pother?

The witches rejoice at this triumph of unfeeling triviality; and the Sorceress foretells the destruction of Carthage in an aria in ceremonial dotted rhythm! Then they all sing a rigid, fierce dance-song, "Destruction's our delight." Played maestoso, this would be imposing in its massive homophony, for rhythm, harmony and modulatory scheme are clear and simple. Played and hissed as fast as possible it becomes the more sinister for being a positive inverted. The witches and sailors significantly dance *together*, for the evil is that the World cannot comprehend the realities of passion.

Then follows the final interview between Dido and "lost Aeneas," which returns to the here-and-now of arioso. Dido begins by saying that no human agency can help her, so she must appeal to "earth and heaven" (high G). But she immediately rounds on herself and says, in effect, that heaven doesn't

4. Most commentators find the conclusion of this act unsatisfactory, because it ends in a different key from the opening (A minor instead of D minor) and with recitative instead of a dance-chorus. Tate in fact provided six lines of gloating for the witches which Purcell probably set (in D minor) as an ironically triumphant gloss on Aeneas's self-pity. It is just possible — though not probable — that Purcell omitted the words on purpose; certainly the opera doesn't seriously suffer from the omission, for the end of this act must appear to some degree bathetic if the story is to make sense.

exist; all she can do is to accept what fate has in store for her. Aeneas enters to make his broken confession of "the gods' decree" (which is really the devil's, of course). His arioso, with its sharpened third in the ascent, flattened third in the descent, is genuinely pathetic, and we are probably meant to feel sorry for him when, after his voice has literally broken before the words "we must part," Dido turns on him in fury. She calls him a "deceitful crocodile," the worse because he isn't man enough to be honest but makes "heaven and gods" (which she knows don't exist) an excuse for his own defection. This is a very English, anti-traditional version of heroism, for she is implying that the only real heroism lies in truth to one's own feelings. It's no use his breaking in to exclaim "By all that's good" because all that's good he has forsworn. It's enough that he should have had the *thought* of deserting her; the unfaith has been committed in his mind, and what's done cannot be undone, certainly not by protestations in perfunctory arpeggios which she parodies in mocking imitations. You have lost love, she says, irrevocably, so you may as well take yourself off to your promised "Empire." Her descending arpeggios to the word "Away" are brusquely ferocious, guillotining Aeneas's rising arpeggios in which he says he'll "stay and love obey." But when she turns to herself and says that she will fly to death, Aeneas abruptly takes himself off. Perhaps he realizes that she, unlike himself, means it, and he is afraid of death because he is afraid of love. There is a kind of savage farce about the scene, but as soon as Aeneas has stumped off, Dido recovers tragic stature. Alone, she says that he had to go (because he betrayed love) and that now he has gone, Death must take her. She "cannot live without him," and the cliché is strictly true in the sense that her realization that his love is not the same as hers kills her. Practically speaking, she could — even if she were not willing, as in real heroic opera, to give him up for Duty — have waited for him to save the State and return to her. But she doesn't want to wait for him because she has discovered that in her sense he is no hero at all, but a sham. It is literally true that Dido is too heroic to live.

So when the chorus sings in solemn ceremonial homophony that "Great minds against themselves conspire" we say, yes, that is so, and is what the opera is about. But when they add "and shun the cure they most desire" we know this is not true, for Aeneas would be no cure for Dido's suffering nor, perhaps, would any mortal man. Aeneas is the traditional man-god gone seedy, as he certainly had in Restoration England; Dido's heroism consists in her being a woman who can still be, emotionally and imaginatively, a queen. The conditions of temporal mortality would seem to be such that private passion can never be completely fulfilled: so the only "cure" for Dido is death. The darkness closes around her as her arioso slowly droops through sobbing

Neapolitan chromaticisms and she welcomes death, her only true lover, in her final aria on a ground bass. Here the bass descends chromatically in the ceremonial rhythm of the chaconne which, in the court masque, was a marriage dance. The apparently eternal repetition of the balanced cadences lifts her sorrow beyond the personal. Though her vocal line is as anguished in its sobbing tritones and yearning chromatics as her most fiery passages of arioso, she grows fully to the tragic queen who was presaged in her first song. Her melody describes a grand, slowly arching contour, rising chromatically, falling in relaxed diatonicism, but when she invites us to "remember" her, her melody stays still on repeated D's, and then on high G's. It is significant that she asks us to remember her — as a woman — but to "forget her fate." Unlike Aeneas, she has no self-pity and she blames no one for the wrongs she suffers. What we have to remember is the reality of human passion — perhaps the ultimate reality. We certainly don't forget it as after she has stabbed herself or died of a broken heart, a dissolving chromatic descent spreads through the whole orchestra.

What happens then is interesting for it suggests that against our expectation after Dido's lament, the "ultimate" reality may not be human passion after all. In a sense Purcell takes us back, in the final chorus, to the point he started from in his early string fancies. It is as though, in the orchestral ritornello that concludes the lament, sensuous chromatic passion — the essence of Dido herself — melts away, to be succeeded by strict vocal polyphony, a four-part canon, moving diatonically, mainly by step, sung by a chorus of Cupids. They are, of course, gods of love and also the plump fruits of love that a paradise of sensuality was liable to leave around, and they scatter the sexual rose upon Dido, as Belinda had said they would in her "Fear no danger" song. But Dido is dead and Aeneas is absent so the Cupids become also baroque cherubs on a tomb who sing like Christian angels of the old world. This is quite different from anything in Blow's elegiacs; again Purcell ends with a nostalgic reference to a world outside the present. Human passion, and in the most literal sense sexual love, is the point we start from, but we end with the admission that the craving of the heart and senses is inappeasable. So we wish we were innocent angels before the Fall, and on the words "never part" the regular dance rhythm (the only survival in this chorus of the humanist ritual of the masque) breaks into sighs and silence.

EDWARD J. DENT

[*Recitative, Dance, and Rhythm*]†

Professor of Music at Cambridge from 1926 to 1941, Edward J. Dent (1876–
1957) was the learned and urbane father of modern British musicology. Opera
was central to his interests, and his major writings on the subject — which include
books on seventeenth-century English music drama, Alessandro Scarlatti, and
Mozart — arose from his pioneering stage productions at Cambridge between the
wars. Dent's study of *Dido and Aeneas* now seems somewhat eccentric with its
focus on the recitatives and dances, but, with some justification, he regarded
these aspects as the most remarkable and original features of the opera.

In judging *Dido and Aeneas* as an opera we have to make some allowances for
the restricted conditions in which it had to be performed, but it is more important that we should put ourselves into the normal frame of mind of the
'select audience of parents' who witnessed that first performance by making
some acquaintance with the general run of theatrical entertainments which
they might have seen on other days. It is surprising how well the opera holds
together in spite of all its shortcomings in construction; recent performances
have often shown how convincingly effective it is even to a modern audience
utterly unfamiliar with the traditions of its own period. That complete certainty of effect is due entirely to Purcell's individual genius; but to say that
does not sum up the whole problem. German critics who have seen *Dido and
Aeneas* on the stage characterize it as 'Shakespearean'; and in the mouth of a
German this epithet carries perhaps more admiration than it would in
England. A more detailed analysis of the opera will explain to a large extent
the technical methods by which Purcell secured the intensity of his dramatic
expression; and it is important that we should investigate these methods carefully, because Purcell's principles are in the main equally applicable to operatic composition in our own day.

Purcell's experiment, in spite of its obvious indebtedness to French and
Italian sources, is a work such as no foreign composer could ever have written.
It conforms to no tradition; it has no sense of style; but it is saved from falling

† From *Foundations of English Opera* (Cambridge: Cambridge University Press, 1928), pp.
187–196. Reprinted with permission.

into the merely picturesque by its robust directness. It is also quite original in
its treatment of the chorus, though Purcell's real genius for dramatic choral
writing was not fully developed until later. But although for the most part the
chorus in *Dido and Aeneas* does no more than repeat exactly the airs sung by
the ubiquitous Belinda, its presence is constantly felt as a factor in the drama,
and in some places the mere suppression of Belinda's solos would give to the
choruses an unexpected and striking individuality. We must regard Belinda
in fact not as a definite person, but merely as a chorus leader, like the miscel-
laneous nymphs who start the choral movements of *The Fairy Queen*. In two
choruses, 'Cupid only throws the dart' (Act I) and 'With drooping wings' (Act
III), we find more individuality of choral treatment, more definite suggestion
of gesture and movement, and we shall see this sense of the stage more conspicuously developed in the later operas.

It is naturally in the recitative that *Dido and Aeneas* is most remarkable,
since, being the only real opera which Purcell ever wrote, it furnished his only
occasion for writing musical dialogue of a genuinely human and dramatic
character. Purcell's recitative is very obviously derived from the Italian chamber cantatas; this is shown by his expressive employment of florid passages,
and his tendency to measured *arioso* rather than to free declamation on an
almost stationary bass, as in Italian *recitativo secco* of the operatic type. Purcell never relaxes the sense of rhythm; his recitatives, like Mozart's, must be
sung on a general basis of strict time. He does not even permit himself that
common Italian formula, the dominant-tonic cadence independent of the
general rhythm, which is scattered all over the works of Bach and Handel, to
say nothing of the Italians, and which to the average reader is the most characteristic and the most annoying feature of recitatives. Nor does Purcell ever
consider that recitative absolves him from the restrictions of key any more
than from those of rhythm. The recitative in Act I 'Whence could so much
virtue spring?' is a good example of his methods. The harmonies of Dido's first
quatrain are as regularly disposed as the accent of the verse, simple in the
extreme, yet always rhythmical; above them the declamation is forcible, the
melody expressive, with a wide compass and rich variety of rhythm. To the
modern reader perhaps the most striking features are the free alternation of
major and minor modes in the same key of C, the bold *coloratura*, and the
sudden burst of energy, heightened by its contrasting bass, in the concluding
bar. Belinda answers in a gentler mood, moving through new keys — G minor,
E flat and A flat, all untouched by Dido — and ending in suspense on the dominant; Dido leads the music back to the original tonality with a long ascending
scale in broken rhythm that brings the whole movement to its emotional climax just before the end. The whole recitative is one continuous and logically

constructed piece of music, beautiful and expressive even if no words were
sung to it; yet the declamation is perfect, and every emotional point is seized
with the most subtle delicacy and certainty.

The recitative of the Sorceress may appear at first less successful. The
Sorceress has not the same human emotions to express. She is a type, not an
individual. She is accompanied by the orchestra and Purcell requires the help
of the orchestra to obtain the necessary 'atmosphere'. He seems to have had in
this scene a prophetic vision of German romantic opera. The storm is suggested by the instrumental introduction and the Sorceress seems slowly and
gradually to disengage herself from the storm, as if she became gradually visible out of the darkness which envelops the scene. Her invocation of the witches
is almost a monotone; Purcell allows the words to dominate the music except
just at those closing bars in which she suddenly bursts out with unconcealed
exultation at the thought of the horrible things which she intends to do. Just
as Dido throughout the first act stands out from the rest as the one person on
the stage whose emotions are genuine and heart-felt, so the Sorceress stands
out grimly self-controlled and intent on her fell purpose against the crowd of
attendant witches who burst in upon her riotous and undisciplined.

The third scene brings yet a different type of recitative. Dido is on the
stage the whole time, with never a word to say until the storm begins. She has
two short lines to sing:

> The skies are clouded! Hark how thunder
> Rends the mountain oaks asunder!

Here again Purcell achieves a clear and definite musical form, at the
same time giving us the contrast between her first half-whispered sentence
and the outburst of terrified *coloratura* which follows. The recitative between
the Spirit and Aeneas suffers musically from the loss of the concluding
witches' chorus. The idea of ending the scene with Aeneas' agony is certainly
very dramatic, but the fact of the recitative ending in A minor instead of leading back to the key of D minor in which the act began leads me to suspect that
Purcell originally intended to write a chorus or dance of witches in D minor,
and either discarded it or abandoned the idea, unfortunately without rewriting the close of the preceding recitative. The dialogue, simple as it is, contains
many admirable points. The quick interruption of Aeneas 'To-night?' is
Tate's invention; Purcell gives it additional effect by repeating the same
notes, E, B, when the Spirit repeats the word. The severe dignity of the Spirit
is balanced by the firm resolution of Aeneas as he answers him; then comes a
pause — one of those pauses so frequent in Purcell's recitatives, pauses which
thanks to the system of accompanying recitative on the harpsichord can be

drawn out almost indefinitely in order to allow the actor to change his position and expression. The final soliloquy of Aeneas is another case where Purcell in a recitative covers a wide range of emotion. It is wider here than in
Dido's dialogue with Belinda; but as in that case the whole movement is held
together by rhythmical balance and careful distribution of key.

Purcell reaches his greatest heights in the long dialogue between Dido
and the departing Aeneas in Act III. As on a previous occasion he begins with
a tonic pedal, a favourite device of Italian chamber cantatas, though in opera
it had hardly been used since the days of Peri and Monteverdi. Note how Purcell in setting the threefold repetition of the words 'earth and heaven' con-
trives to use the same notes in each case, but with different basses, planned so
as to increase the emotional effect, an effect still further heightened by the
harsh and scornful minor ninth on the last 'earth'. Aeneas speaks in subdued
and broken tones; Dido bursts in upon him with fury, again making her emotional point by the repetition of and return to a single emphatic note. A
moment later she does the same thing:

Aeneas.   By all that's good —
Dido.   By all that's good! No more
            All that's good you have foreswore.

In each case the words 'all that's good' are set to the same notes; the third
time, however, the bass moves, so as to make a very harsh 'false relation' of
B natural against B flat. Yet again Dido employs the device, in the phrase
'Away, away' repeated for the last time quite by itself after the two have joined
in a duet of protestations.

Aeneas has nothing but recitative to sing, except for a few bars of measured duet with Dido in the last scene. The reason for this is doubtless the fact
that Aeneas was the only character acted by a man at the first performance.
His part is written in the tenor clef in the Tenbury MS., all the others being in
the treble. No doubt the Spirit and the Sailor were both sung by girls in the
school. * * *

The dances are among the most interesting features of the opera. These
also were introduced in view of the special conditions of the first performance,
but they are a valuable ingredient of the opera even now, provided that they
are rightly interpreted. Those of the first scene do not call for comment. The
Echo dance at the end of the second scene is confusing if printed continuously
as in the MS., but in the Oxford vocal score it is set out as for two orchestras.
This explains its form at once, and it can be made very effective in performance if care is taken to secure a right balance and an exact synchronization
of the two groups of players, one in front and the other behind the scenes.

The amusing thing about the echoes is that they never reproduce the exact harmony of the original phrases; this ingenious device gives them a delightfully fantastic character, as if the human witches on the stage were answered by spirit dancers who strangely distort their movements. The sailors' dance, like the whole scene of the sailors, is irrelevant to the plot, but it is a welcome irrelevance and its boisterous gaiety prepares well for the tragic scene which follows. The sailors' dance ought certainly to be danced by men, and by men alone, as a definite exhibition of sailors dancing for the amusement of the crowd on the stage. The second dance (after the scene of the witch) is more difficult to understand. It is evidently an imitation of the capricious dances of Locke such as occur in *Cupid and Death* (Dance of the Satyr and Apes). The curious misprint of the original libretto adds to the confusion. The whole scene will become much clearer if we bear in mind the seventeenth-century view of witches. Witches in those days may or may not have possessed supernatural powers, but they were undoubtedly real human beings whom one might meet any day. The witches in *Dido and Aeneas* are therefore not to be represented as spirits; they are old women, and probably young ones too, such as might quite naturally be found among the crowd in the neighbourhood of the harbour. Duffett's parodies of the operas of Shadwell show us plainly what sort of characters they were in normal life. The first section of this dance may well represent the gestures of the witches who are planning the ruin of the sailors; the second (3/4) will suit either 'Jack o' lanthorn' — a ragged child personating a will-o'-the-wisp — or the more dangerously attractive 'inchanteresses'; while the third section will serve to accompany a scene of general quarrelling, tumult and confusion. * * *

What gives the whole opera its intense dramatic force is its swiftness of thought. Purcell expresses in ten bars emotions for which Bach or Handel would have required a hundred. For concentration of energy *Dido and Aeneas* stands alone among operas of all time. It is well that we should understand its technical methods. Purcell makes his effect by purely musical means. He has not merely the feeling for expressive harmony; he has a technical command of melody which enables him to balance unequal groups of bars, phrases of five bars where we should expect four, groups of three phrases where we might expect an even number. A good example is the chorus 'Harm's our delight'; it consists of a five-bar phrase ending with a definite cadence balanced by a group of ten bars, which divide not into five and five (in spite of the repetition of melody) but into six and four. A scheme such as this is only manageable by a composer who can conceive of his entire movement as a complete rhythmic whole; and we must feel this movement as a complete rhythmic whole if we are to sing it properly. In the recitatives the swiftness is obtained by the vigorous and accurate declamation of the words. Here the English language is an immense help; but the singer must contribute his share of the labour. A firm sense of rhythm must be established at once; when this is secured the singer will find that he can ultimately allow himself an amount of freedom in pace which would be impossible if he began the recitative with the oratorio-singer's reverent disregard of rhythm.

Dramatic as is Purcell's type of recitative, it must be admitted that the Italians were quite right in confining its model to the chamber. No composer could have kept it up, no audience could have borne the strain if it had been employed continuously throughout the dialogue of a full-sized Italian opera. Purcell could employ it here, and here only, because it forms only a small part —less than one-third—of the entire work, and the entire work is about one-third of the length of the average Italian opera.

In this matter Purcell and his fellow-workers were probably wiser than they knew. They had the choice between short opera of a highly concentrated quality, and long opera in which there must inevitably have been many tracts of comparatively little interest. The long operas of Lulli were held together more by the literary form of Quinault's drama than by any intrinsic musical method; the Italian operas were either shapeless masses of disconnected episodes, as at Venice, or formal dramas sung to more formal arias as at Naples. But Purcell, strong as was his sense of form, did not yet possess the musical technique to organize a whole opera on a large scale, and since the English poets of the period were utterly incapable of doing anything to help him in this direction, *Dido and Aeneas* never had a successor.

ROBERT E. MOORE

[Dido and Aeneas *and Later Opera*]†

Purcell's only opera stands in isolation from the baroque mainstream, and it also seems to have had no significant influence on any composer before Benjamin Britten. But Robert E. Moore in his monograph *Henry Purcell & the Restoration Theatre* notices how uncannily *Dido* anticipates dramatic techniques of later tragic operas. His book, the first devoted exclusively to Purcell's major stage works, also includes an invaluable study of baroque aesthetics.

The stark simplification of Virgil's story is highly significant. Purcell and Tate evidently believed that the plot should be cut down to its barest bones, a decision very uncharacteristic of the seventeenth century. The modest conditions of the performance obviously influenced this plan, but more important is something Purcell came to realize which exhibits his genius in the most revealing light, and which had vast implications for his subsequent work. This is simply that the intensity of tragic art is attained through spartan concentration, through the stripping away of all flamboyant and episodic intrigue, in fact, through bald austerity. The recognition of what may seem a self-evident truth has always been enormously difficult to the composer of serious opera, and of course even more difficult has been the practical fulfilment of the ideal.

Purcell may possibly have come upon it by accident, nor is *Dido* by any means a flawless work, but the fact remains that he has created the first modern tragic opera. To enjoy it fully demands no acquaintance with an older style, as do the operas of Monteverdi. Seventy-five years later Gluck, working in close collaboration with his librettist Calzabigi, quite deliberately endeavored to free his work of all episode, to concentrate on the kind of simple yet highly-charged emotional situation that we find in *Dido*. To this kind of simplicity the greatest tragic operas, like *Norma* or *Otello* or *Tristan*, always cling unshakeably. It is the interminable and elaborately stylized Italian operas of the seventeenth and eighteenth centuries, seen at their least tedious in Handel and Alessandro Scarlatti, and the blood and thunder school of the

† From *Henry Purcell & the Restoration Theatre* (London: Heinemann, 1961), pp. 41–6. Reprinted with permission.

220

nineteenth, epitomized by Meyerbeer, which felt the need of incessant thrills to keep up the pitch. An opera like *Dido* exposes their meretricious effects; if the intensity of feeling, and of course the composer's technical proficiency, be great enough, the music itself will take complete charge. Almost nothing in the way of stage action happens in *Dido* or in *Orfeo* or in *Tristan*. * * * Having decided upon a severely reduced scale of action, and one not without its perils, for Aeneas becomes all but a blank, Purcell then had to meet the task of organizing his opera. Dido begins anguished and ends dead, yet some way must be found of attuning all of the work to tragedy and at the same time avoiding three acts of inspissated gloom. Purcell had both the French and Italian model to draw upon, and in the usual English manner effected a happy compromise between the two. *Dido* is built around the choral and ballet plan of Lullian opera where the dance serves as a link between the narrative portions and the scenes of spectacle, but to this he adds arias which are clearly differentiated from the recitative after the manner of Venetian and Neapolitan opera where dance and chorus were negligible. * * *

Dido, as I hope presently to show, is an uncanny anticipation of the Gluck ideal three-quarters of a century before *Orfeo* (1762). Probably working from no theory but guided by a remarkable dramatic taste and instinct, Purcell solved most of the difficulties of the two levels [i.e., recitative and aria]. It is to the chorus that he turns for his strongest unifying factor, and here we detect at once the strong influence of the English masque of which the chorus had been the musical centre. It has been noted that they perform a role in *Dido* analogous to that of the chorus of Greek tragedy, entering into the action as participants and commenting upon it as observers. They end each scene[1] and make possible the sublime apotheosis of the opera. Even stronger links with the masque are the dances which weave in and out of the work. Though they often reflect the piquant rhythms of Lully, unlike the French model they are always dramatically relevant and significant. In the midst of these ensembles and intimately connected with them, Dido herself is firmly planted as the centre of the first and last acts, while the middle portion of the opera emphasizes Aeneas and the witches. The chorus is integrated even more strongly by having as its leader the other principal character, Belinda, who is the traditional confidante of neo-classical tragedy, and the heroine's sister as well.

From an exclusively musical point of view Purcell strengthens the formal unity of the work by constructing as a kind of polar centre to each act an im-

---

1. What looks like an exception, the end of Act II, is only partially so, for the libretto contains a closing chorus which Purcell either did not set or for which the music has been lost.

posing aria on a ground bass. Furthermore, he maintains throughout the opera a carefully considered plan of key relationships which give significance to a succession of short separate movements and heighten the impression of the musical whole.

The foregoing remarks will suggest, even before we look at the music, a certain stately simplicity in Purcell's dramaturgy which is indeed characteristic of most baroque opera. A recent critic has summarized the position by saying, 'The baroque musical continuity was formed by a process of unfolding rather than by dramatic development, but it was possible to arrange a grand and particularly intense sort of drama by the placing of such musical blocks.'[2] This is not to say that their plots, like *Dido*'s, were simple, for they were fairly bursting with inane complications; rather he is speaking of the musical conception of each scene. These devices are very important to Purcell, for since the time of Mozart operatic composers have depended heavily upon two resources that were unavailable to him, the vocal ensemble and the enormous resources of the modern orchestra.

The ensemble, in which a number of characters express their varying emotions simultaneously, is an outgrowth of the sonata form developed by Haydn and Mozart, the form upon which our modern symphonic style is based. In nearly all Mozart operas the emotional climaxes are concentrated not upon a solo aria or duet (except for the chorus the limit of Purcell's artillery), but upon the mingled voices, *molto agitato*, of all the principals. A striking example of how different is the effect of the two methods can be seen by comparing with Purcell the episode in Berlioz's *Trojans* where Dido and Aeneas reach the point of declaring their love. Purcell is confined to a number of very short movements of increasing intensity: Belinda urges, then the chorus, then Aeneas, then Belinda and chorus again, and so on. At the climax Dido herself says nothing — 'Fate forbids what you pursue', well before the end of the scene, is her last line — and we are left to gather that she yields only from the words of the final chorus, and in performance of course from her own miming. But Berlioz, after a series of lesser episodes, moves into a massive quintet in which each character most dramatically expresses what is at stake for himself as well as for the others. The concerns of Dido, Aeneas, and Anna (Purcell's Belinda) may be imagined, but those of Dido's minister of state for the future of Carthage reveal something of the scale of Berlioz's subject in comparison with Purcell's. Not he nor even Gluck could possibly have written an opera called *The Trojans*, but their resources were admirably suited to a work on Dido and Aeneas. The quintet and the following septet

2. Joseph Kerman: *Opera as Drama*, p. 77.

are the climax of the act; after the choice has there been faced and the decision reached, the other principals fade from the scene, leaving the lovers to an
ecstatic duet whose mood is not torrid passion but rather serene lyricism. * * *

The other limitation in Purcell's dramaturgy Gluck was able to overcome
by the developments of the intervening three-quarters of a century. In the
dedicatory letter to *Alceste* he remarks that the combinations of instruments
should be controlled by the passion of the situation. When one notes that Purcell's orchestration is merely for two violins, viola, bass, and continuo, the tale
is told. The libretto twice mentions 'gitters' for dance movements, but the
score does not provide for them. In his later operas his palette is larger—
trumpets, oboes, an occasional bassoon—and his range of orchestral colour
within these instruments is amazing. But it is not until the abolition of the
continuo, the system by which the filling out of the harmonic background was
given over to the harpsichordist, that the dramatic employment of the orchestra could really begin. One need only think of the short-cuts and compressions
that Wagner or Strauss can effect by a mere phrase or theme in the orchestra,
the functions of reminiscence or foreboding that are performed, effects that
the poetical dramatist cannot convey by words, to see how the modern orchestra functions as a character in the drama in a manner undreamed of even by
Gluck or Mozart, let alone Purcell.

Yet with all these limitations imposed by his time and place, it must be
repeated that Purcell has composed the first modern opera, a music drama
completely coherent and self-sufficient, which means that the dramatic artic-
ulation is provided entirely by the music. Unlike its greatest operatic prede-
cessor, Monteverdi's *Orfeo*, *Dido and Aeneas* is written in an idiom entirely
familiar to everyone. With the possible exception of the part played by the
witches, there is not the slightest need for apologies or for any explanations of
an extra-musical nature.

JOSEPH KERMAN

[*A Glimmer from the Dark Ages*]†

Joseph Kerman is baroque opera's severest critic. Fortunately, *Dido and Aeneas* is well outside the various seventeenth- and eighteenth-century traditions for which he has so little use. But, as the following extract from the essential book on opera shows, this is not the only reason he awards Purcell the laurels.

Dido is a unique work, innocent of any indigenous operatic tradition, written not for the *roi soleil* but for a young ladies' academy, and dashed off with a cheerful incorrectness which would have horrified Lully. *Dido* is a miniature; like Gluck's *Orfeo*, it dodges the cruel problem of making a full evening's entertainment for a court that demands a decent cut of splendor. Its dramatic perfection is nonetheless in Lully's cast. In spite of the critical anomaly caused by the inclusion of real arias, its dramaturgy is basically determined by chorus, dance, and formalized recitative.

Little enough of Vergil remains, perhaps. Dido is drastically simplified, and Aeneas is made into a complete booby; the sense of cosmic forces at play is replaced by the machination of an outrageous set of Restoration witches. The simplification of Dido's character, however, is not without a resulting gain in concentration, and the chorus of her courtiers is admirably Sophoclean in spirit. They give, first of all, an intimate impression of the stake of Carthage in Dido's suicide. Furthermore the carefully worked-out progress of the chorus, in relation to Dido, illuminates and actually defines the personal tragedy.

The first scene contains five short choruses led by Belinda (Vergil's Anna), who doubles as chorus-leader and *confidante*. Repeatedly they encourage the proposed match between Dido and Aeneas, finally calling for the Triumphs of Love and the Revels of Cupids as they go off to the hunt. Their trivial, hearty enthusiasm is at odds with the sentiment of Dido's single apprehensive aria—though this too, perhaps, speaks as yet in the accents of courtly convention.

† From *Opera as Drama* (New York: Vintage Books, 1956), pp. 56–61. Copyright © 1956 by Joseph Kerman. Reprinted by permission of Alfred A. Knopf, Inc.

[Act II, scene i] shows the plotting of the witches, who substitute for Jupiter and Venus in hastening Aeneas' desertion. Dido and her train, of course, know nothing of this, but when we see them in the country in the next [scene] their song has a strange melancholy, which the "Triumphing Dance" had not led us to expect. The scene opens with what might be described as a masque fragment, a graceful, solemn little suite of song and dance to entertain the Queen while Aeneas hunts. But it is the story of Actaeon and Diana that comes to mind, in these "lonesome vales" which Venus had been said to favor. The storm dispels the chorus, and — more decorously than in Vergil — Dido too. Aeneas is left to hear the witches' "trusty elf, / In form of Mercury himself," to wrestle with himself cursorily, and to accede to the demands of fate.

In Act III the witches appear again, with a rude chorus of the departing sailors, whose traditional sanguine song of abandoning their girls practically puts the words into Aeneas' mouth. After a violent scene with Dido, he leaves, and she prepares to mount her funeral pyre. Two choruses exquisitely frame Dido's famous aria, "When I am laid in earth." As Aeneas goes, she sings two lines in recitative: "But death, alas, I cannot shun; / Death must come when he is gone"; then the chorus, gravely silent during the quarrel, comments: "Great minds against themselves conspire / And shun the cure they most desire." This platitudinous couplet is like those with which the Greek chorus often breaks into a highly charged dialogue. It is all of thirteen bars long, but set in place with a brilliant sense of the drama. It provides a release of tension; a sudden new vantage point, an outside point of balance from which to gauge Dido's grief; a delicate transition from the stabbing dialogue of the quarrel to the lyric pace demanded by the conclusion; a tonal preparation for the ending g minor; and a great passage of time, a lifetime of decision for Dido. The luminous B♭ chords at the start turn to g minor and to quiet repetitions of a poignant figure in the ending phrase. From the flippancy of Act I and the vaguely motivated melancholy of Act II, the chorus comes finally to gravity and awareness.

This puts foolish Aeneas and the pantomime witches out of mind; Dido's supreme aria can follow. By the clock, it occupies approximately one-twelfth of the time of the whole opera, and comes with particular spaciousness after the economy of the earlier action. No operatic climax has ever been approached with more direct strength, in a more genuinely classic dramatic rhythm. By relying heavily on a lyric aria, of course, Purcell stepped out of Lully's convention. Lully has his "*airs*," but they are the simplest and most reticent things, comparable to Belinda's little songs in *Dido and Aeneas*. Though French recitative always tends to arioso, the *airs* sound like slightly melodious recitative. The French would not accept the frank Italian convention whereby words and reason yield, at a dramatic crux, to the emotional expression of music handled in its own terms.

* * * Purcell was no great master of musical form—nor was anyone else in 1690—but he was a specialist at the "ground bass," a naïve and sometimes tedious formal device which is, however, magnificently apposite to Dido's dying lament. Its feeling stems from obsessive repetition: the bass of this aria consists exclusively of nine statements of a single figure, without transposition or variation of any kind. As a matter of fact, this particular descending, depressive bass figure was common musical property. Cavalli employed it regularly for laments; there is one for Hecuba in his *Didone*. Lully worked it into the scene of mourning for Alceste. Bach used it at the *Crucifixus* of the B-minor Mass, and elsewhere. Purcell achieved an especially leaden effect by stretching it into a five-bar unit rather than the more usual four or six, dragging on the dominant D. For variety, he made the vocal line overlap ingeniously the cadences in the bass, as is shown in the musical example. The harmonies change only slightly with successive repetitions of the bass—until the climax, where on Dido's ultimate cry of "ah" the dominant major harmony is replaced by the modal-sounding, bleak minor chord (compare the first and sixth bars in the example; notice also the slow clashing of dissonant seconds

below). In context this simple harmonic effect is tragic, and I use the term in as pure a sense as I know. Then, as Dido ends her song and mounts the pyre, the orchestra runs down a great slow chromatic scale derived from the bass pattern, closing the aria with a sense of quiet excruciation — or rather, breaking through to the concluding choral elegy. The very simplicity of the form, with its unyielding, uncomprehending bass, seems to stress, magnify, and force the insistant grief of Dido's situation.

What is so exactly in the Italian aesthetic, and out of the French, is that the whole piece is strung out to two trivial lines of verse; and that the great climax on the d-minor chord comes on a single syllable "ah" — a pre-verbal cry. Purcell understood that this could be infinitely more expressive than Lully's most elegantly declaimed Alexandrine. But he also understood something better still: how to organize arias into a total, coherent dramatic form. The lament does not end, but flows into the wonderful final chorus, the most elaborately extended in the opera. To a solemn choral dance, "Cupids appear in the clouds o'er her tomb"; Cupids, though, "with drooping wings"; Dido's agony softens and deepens out towards the audience through the mourning community on the stage. All through the opera Dido and the courtiers advance and converge, and at the end the courtiers, grown worthy of Dido's government, can take the stage after her death with full consciousness of the tragedy.

Few operas use a chorus so beautifully, or so integrally. But it is worth emphasizing that the convention employed was well within Lully's ken, and one that might easily be pooh-poohed as undramatic. The plan was simply to end each scene, and to begin as many as possible, with a community song and dance. (Nahum Tate even provided a chorus at the end of Act II, though Purcell does not appear to have composed it.) *Le merveilleux* was as imperative in a school play as at the court of Louis XIV. It presents its challenge to the dramatist; Purcell was able to meet it.

With recitative he was able to do less, though like Lully he devoted a great deal of attention to it. It is very carefully written, and vigorously declaimed, but impersonal, courtly, and bombastic; all that is presented is the shell, the form of passion. From Dido's recitatives we can tell that she is every inch a queen, but only from her arias can we become interested in her as a person. (There are moments, though: "Thy hand, Belinda," prior to the great aria.) Where Purcell trusted his recitative most, it let him down most seriously: in the long recitative for Aeneas after he is warned by the Elf, at the end of Act II. This was supposed to make a rousing curtain and to give Aeneas dramatic dimension comparable to that of the Queen; the method is Monteverdi's and Lully's. But Aeneas remains a nonentity — without destroying the drama, fortunately. Only in the highly organized accompanied recitative for the Sorceress, "Wayward sisters," whose very *ritornello* foreshadows the coming line in the voice, is Purcell really at the height of his power.

JOHN BUTTREY

[*A Cautionary Tale*]†

The purpose of the original article from which the following is extracted was to narrow the date of the premiere of *Dido and Aeneas*, which was long in doubt, to the spring of 1689. John Buttrey's evidence embraces the far larger topic of political allegory in English opera and shows *Dido* to have been an instrument of propaganda during turbulent times. His ideas about the political function of English opera—developed at length in his 1967 Cambridge Ph.D. dissertation—were slow to gain acceptance among British musicologists, which is surprising in light of what has long been known about the related function of the prologues to Lully's *tragédies en musique*.

To understand how the English people felt in the late seventeenth century, one must go back to the time when Henry VIII abandoned the Church of Rome and established himself at the head of the English Church. In doing this he started a controversy that was to rage fiercely for generations, and the religious strife which followed the deaths of Henry and his young son, Edward VI, was burned into the memories of the English people. Indeed, for the next two centuries, the anniversary of Elizabeth I's accession was venerated because it represented the return to Protestantism after the blood-bath of Mary Tudor's reign. What is more, the recollections of that disastrous period were responsible for rousing the horror against Catholics in 1605 at the attempt to murder James I by the Gunpowder Plot. They were also the source of some of the fanaticism that fomented into the Civil War, when Charles I tried to foist an hierarchical church on to the Scottish Presbyterians. Nor did the Commonwealth which followed the War put an end to religious hatreds. After the

† From "Dating Purcell's Dido and Aeneas," *Proceedings of the Royal Musical Association*, 96 (1967–8), 52–60. Reprinted with permission.

Restoration of the Monarchy in 1660, Charles II had a difficult time maintaining a balance between the religious parties in the kingdom. The King himself was a secret adherent of the Church of Rome, and had pledged himself to Louis XIV that he would turn England back to Catholicism. But his experience during the Civil War made Charles realise that any such move would cause him to lose the crown, so he vacillated and managed to disguise his beliefs until he finally accepted conversion to the Roman Church on his deathbed.

But then the trouble began, for his brother, James II, who succeeded him in 1685, had been an acknowledged Catholic for years. Furthermore, he showed great foolishness in flaunting his beliefs at that time, for his subjects were being terrified by the news from across the Channel. By the revocation of the Edict of Nantes, Protestants in France had become branded as heretics and were being slaughtered by the hundred. Yet, despite their fear, the English people were prepared to tolerate James as long as his elder daughter, Mary, remained the heir presumptive. She was James's daughter by his first wife, and had been brought up in the English Church. She was also married to William, the Protestant Prince of Orange. William (as a grandson of Charles I of England) had long believed that he himself might one day inherit the English throne. So, since he was married to James's heir, the situation seemed assured. But in 1688, despite expectations to the contrary, James's second wife gave birth to a healthy son, and Princess Mary was displaced from direct succession. Yet many people were convinced that the birth was a fraud designed to reestablish a Catholic monarchy in England. Even the Princess Mary believed that she had been cheated out of her inheritance. The result was that prominent Englishmen petitioned the Prince of Orange to intervene in the nation's affairs. So, having gathered an army together, William set sail for the English coast. But hardly had the fleet set out than it was driven back to Holland in the teeth of a gale. For five days the storm raged, and only when it abated was William able to cross the Channel and land in the south of England. James, realising that all was lost, fled with his family to France. Thereupon, William was triumphantly received in London, and proceeded to negotiate with Parliament regarding the accession to the throne. Several months later, Princess Mary followed her husband to England, and in February 1689 she and William accepted the crown as equal and joint rulers, for William refused to act merely as regent, or allow his wife to retain the sole regnal power.

This is the point where one can understand the reference which D'Urfey made in his Epilogue to *Dido and Aeneas*. The remark, 'Rome may allow strange tricks', refers to the supposedly fraudulent birth of a son to James and his Catholic queen. Such a comment could only have been made after William and Mary had ascended the English throne. It has therefore been conceded that the opera must have been performed sometime after February 1689 but before the Autumn of that year when D'Urfey's Epilogue appeared in print.

Turning now to the opera itself, it was Edward J. Dent who pointed out that the text had in fact been based by Nahum Tate on one of his earlier plays.[1] This play was called *Brutus of Alba*, but in his Preface to the play-book, Tate made the following statement:

> . . . I would not have the reader surprised to find this Tragedy bear some resemblance with the passages of the Fourth Book of the AENEIDS, for I had begun and finished it under the names of DIDO and AENEAS but was wrought by advice of some friends to transform it to the dress it now wears. They told me it would appear arrogant to attempt any characters that had been written by the incomparable VIRGIL . . .

So Tate altered Aeneas to Brutus and transformed Dido into the Queen of Syracuse instead of Carthage, but the plot still retains its likeness to the story found in *The Aeneid*.

Yet it transpires that when Tate decided to rename the characters, his choice of alternatives was no irresponsible matter. If one consults Geoffrey of Monmouth's *Historia regum Britanniae*, one finds there a definite connection between Aeneas and Brutus of Alba. This 'History of the Kings of Britain' was written by the monk Geoffrey of Monmouth in the first half of the twelfth century, and is of interest to us because Geoffrey intended his work as a British sequel to Virgil's epic. This is clear from the way that the book begins. According to Geoffrey of Monmouth, when Aeneas fled after the Trojan War, he arrived in Italy, married the daughter of the king, and finally seized the throne. (Incidentally, in his anxiety to get on with the tale, Geoffrey does not mention the affair with Dido, but presumably he expected his readers to be so familiar with Virgil that they would take this episode for granted.) After Aeneas died, says Geoffrey, his son Ascanius succeeded him, and founded on the banks of the Tiber a city called Alba. Ascanius was succeeded by his son, Silvius, who in turn had a son called Brutus. (So, according to Geoffrey of Monmouth, Brutus of Alba was the great-grandson of Aeneas the Trojan.) When Brutus reached manhood, the goddess Diana prophesied that he should sail to an island named Albion, which lay beyond the realms of Gaul, and there he would finally refound the city of Troy. Brutus did as he was told, and all this took place. The island was called Britain, after Brutus's own name,

---

1. *Foundations of English Opera*, Cambridge, 1928, p. 178.

and Troynovant (i.e., London) was founded on the banks of the Thames. Then, having established this, Geoffrey spends the rest of his book in tracing the lineal descent of Brutus through the kings of Britain (Locrinus, King Lear, Vortigern, and so on), reaching the climax of his work with the exploits of King Arthur. Finally, Geoffrey finishes at the point where Cadwallader gives up the crown to go to Rome, and a heavenly voice prophesies that Britons shall one day rule again in these islands.

Now Virgil's purpose in writing *The Aeneid* was to link the glories of ancient Troy to those of the Roman Empire. So it appears that Geoffrey of Monmouth's intention was to transplant this link and connect Troy with Britain, by means of Aeneas's great-grandson. We have no difficulty now in recognising Geoffrey's *Historia* as a work of fiction, yet, for centuries after it was written, this book was taken as the true record of British kingship. As a result, innumerable writers found it convenient to turn to Geoffrey's account of the royal line in order to back up the claims of certain monarchs to the English throne. For this reason, various aspects of the legend can be found recurring again and again to substantiate political claims.

This was particularly the case during the reigns of the Tudors and Stuarts, and it is illuminating to trace such instances of how the myth was used. For example, when Henry, Earl of Richmond, killed Richard III in 1485 at the end of the Wars of the Roses, and succeeded him as Henry VII, this was regarded in some quarters as usurpation. So, to bolster his claim, Henry declared himself descended from Cadwallader and the Arthurian line, and argued that true British kingship had been restored in his person. He even christened his eldest son Arthur, to emphasize the point.[2] But the unfortunate Prince Arthur died before he could inherit the throne, and it passed to his younger brother, Henry VIII. Henry's contribution to history lay in the field of religious politics. But, as far as the crown was concerned, he left a son and two daughters to succeed him to the throne. It was then during the reign of Elizabeth I that the legend came to light again. Only one flaw existed to mar the devotion of the people to their Queen, and that was Elizabeth's refusal to marry and provide the nation with an heir. Yet even this was turned to her good account. The Queen, they said, was married to her people, and her virginity a sign that she intended to keep this vital bond secure. Once again the British legend was brought in to bolster this belief, for it may be seen in two portraits of the Queen which have, in the background, symbolic pillars illustrating the Dido and Aeneas story. As Dr. Strong points out, the

2. Edward Halle, *The Union of the . . . famelies of Lancastre and Yorke*, London, 1548 (reprinted 1809), pp. 423, 428.

simple analogy is between Aeneas lured from his divine mission by the powers of love, and Elizabeth who, because of her virginity, has refused to be deflected from her path.[3]

When Elizabeth nominated James of Scotland to the English crown, the legend came into use again. James's strongest claim lay in his descent from Henry VII. But many people were impressed that, if James succeeded, England and Scotland would be united under one crown. To them, this seemed a fulfilment of the prophecy in Geoffrey's *Historia* that the British kings would one day return and establish a united kingdom. The number of references to the legend at that time show that the issue was taken very seriously. For instance, in *The Masque at Lord Hay's Marriage* in 1607, Campion introduced the prophecy of Merlin to imply that James was the true successor of Arthur.[4] But even such skilful propaganda could not cover the split in the political structure of the country which grew wider as the reign progressed. Again the trouble was partly religious for, although James was Protestant, his attitude towards Catholic Spain and his emulation of the absolutist monarchy of France brought him into conflict with the House of Commons, most of whose members were Puritans. Then when Charles I succeeded him in 1625, he proceeded to worsen the situation. So there is no need to explain the paucity of references to the Trojan legend during the Civil War and the Commonwealth, when Charles I was beheaded by his own subjects and kingship was abolished by Act of Parliament.

One might well imagine that the Interregnum could have killed belief in this extraordinary prop to British kingship. Yet the legend not only survived, but came into use almost as much as earlier in the century. In fact, the subject of Opera emphatically proves the survival of the legend. Examining the operas that appeared in London at the end of the seventeenth century, there one can see, in their titles alone, that Dryden's *Albion and Albanius* (1685), Tate's *Dido and Aeneas* (1689), Dryden's *King Arthur* (1691), and Powell and Verbruggen's *Brutus of Alba* (1696) all refer to some aspect or another of Geoffrey of Monmouth's *Historia regum Britanniae*. Four such references in eleven years preclude the possibility of coincidence, and here is evidence that the new medium of English opera was not only topical, but that its topicality was concerned with King and State. Yet if we remember that this was the period when determined efforts were being made to re-establish a Catholic monarchy in England, and that Purcell's opera was produced not long after

---

3. Roy C. Strong, *Portraits of Queen Elizabeth I*, Oxford, 1963, p. 68, and Plates 45, 46.
4. Roberta Florence Brinkley, *Arthurian Legend in the Seventeenth Century*, Baltimore, 1932, p. 10.

one such effort had failed, this may help us to see what Tate and Purcell were actually intending.

Previously, the plot of the opera has always been related to *The Aeneid*, but, as I have shown, it is likely that Tate was more influenced by Geoffrey of Monmouth's sequel. Yet, before going on to consider the opera, it is useful to look at the original version of the tale. Since Virgil was trying to link Troy with the Roman Empire, his intention in devising the incident of Dido in his poem was to show that Aeneas was wrong when he fell in love and planned to stay in Carthage. Indeed, the point of the story was that Aeneas had to be reminded of his mission to refound the Trojan line in Italy, not in Africa. So, in *The Aeneid*, it is Jupiter who sends his messenger, Mercury, to bring Aeneas back to his senses; thereby it is the Gods who are made responsible for keeping him to his destiny. As a result, Dido's sacrifice is made subservient to the importance of re-establishing the Trojan heritage at Rome.

I have already shown that, in the reign of Elizabeth I, the story was used to throw light on the Queen's refusal to marry. It is interesting then, to look at the late sixteenth-century play, *Dido, Queen of Carthage* (usually attributed to Marlowe and Nash). Here, the emphasis is thrown on Dido by depicting her as a Circe-like temptress who tries to prevent Aeneas from fulfilling his divine mission. Thus it corresponds to the story as it appears in the two portraits of the Queen, where the purpose was to point out Elizabeth's determination to be faithful to her people. So it is significant that both the play and the portraits date from the same period. But it is important to realise that the point rests, not in equating the Queen with Aeneas, but in the idea of associating Elizabeth with the moral of Aeneas's story.

Another play which is worthy of attention is Tate's earlier essay on the same tale, which he re-named *Brutus of Alba*. This piece was produced in 1678, during the reign of Charles II. At that time, Charles was embroiled in trying to defeat the villainous Earl of Shaftesbury, who, with the help of Charles's illegitimate son, the Duke of Monmouth, was endeavouring to unseat the King and place the crown on Monmouth's head. Tate's play is not difficult to interpret in the light of these events. The story follows Virgil, except that here Tate introduces a designing Syracusan Lord (Monmouth) who seeks to obtain the crown for himself, and employs a Sorceress (Shaftesbury) to help him. To effect their scheme, the Sorceress gives the queen and Brutus a magic potion. As a result, Brutus seduces the queen and dallies with her in Syracuse. But this time he is brought to his senses, not by a messenger from the Gods, but by one of his friends who, rather than stand by and see Brutus forsake his destiny, commits suicide. After this, Brutus sails away to found a kingdom in Albion, while Dido is left to pine from grief and finally takes her life. So once

again we can see that the legend was adapted, not to portray, but to reflect
the events of the time when it was written.

As we have seen in both these plays, the significant points are not those
that correspond to Virgil's epic, but the details wherein the authors digress
from his story. What is more, the same applies in the libretto of the opera
which, as we have seen, was produced in the reign of William and Mary. This
time it is Dido and her position that claims attention, and the refounding of
Troy is made insignificant in comparison to the terrible fate of Carthage. Indeed, the opera reflects the position of the new English queen whose reign
depended upon the support she could claim from her foreign husband.

At the beginning of the opera, the queen is found sunk in melancholy
which she cannot shake off even when chided by her sister. Dido confesses that
she is pining with an emotion she cannot express, and her courtiers guess that
she has fallen in love with the Trojan, Aeneas. When the prince himself
appears and declares his passion, the courtiers approve that the queen should
succumb to his pleading, and that Troy and Carthage should be united.[5] (So,
quite early in the opera, the situation is made plain. In encouraging Dido to
accept Aeneas, the courtiers reveal the vital point of the story: the union of
the two nations.) But unknown to the courtiers, a Sorceress is planning to
destroy the queen out of pure hatred. (There is no mention this time of a
usurper who seeks the crown.) Knowing that Aeneas is bound by fate to make
his way to Italy, the Sorceress plans to confront him during a storm with *one
of her sprites transformed to resemble Mercury*, and charge him sail that
night and abandon Dido. Then, later, during a hunting-scene, the Sorceress's
storm bursts over Dido and Aeneas and, while the queen seeks shelter, the
prince is broached by the false Mercury and given the fraudulent message.
Aeneas, aware of how Dido will react, throws the blame unknowingly on the
Gods, and the Sorceress and her cronies gloat over their success (for they have
tricked Aeneas into deserting the queen). But when Dido learns that Aeneas is
leaving, she is overcome with rage at his treachery. When the prince tries to
account for his behaviour, she spurns his arguments and calls him a hypocrite.
When he innocently offers to defy the Gods, still Dido scorns him for ever
thinking of leaving her. So, with the queen's recriminations ringing in his
ears, Aeneas departs, but as soon as he has gone, Dido feels death approach-
ing her, and after bidding farewell to her sister she dies. (Still little reference

---

5. '. . . The greatest blessing fate can give,
   Our Carthage to secure and Troy revive.
   When monarchs unite, how happy their state,
   They triumph at once on their foes and their fate . . .'

has been made to the refounding of Troy. Instead, the upshot of the deceit brings about Dido's death, and the conclusion of the opera echoes the Sorceress's prophecy: 'Elissa bleeds tonight, and Carthage flames tomorrow'.)

The presence of the witches in the opera has puzzled many people. Because the plot has always been linked with Virgil, these characters are usually considered as Restoration appendages. But this is not the case. Indeed, how can it be when, in the seventeenth century, witches were still being hunted and killed in England. Nor were these romantic witches either, but real human beings who, through superstition, were branded as having infernal powers which brought evil on the heads of others. So, in seventeenth-century drama, whereas the Gods represent the powers of good, sorceresses and witches are symbolic of evil. Again, because of the swift action in Tate's libretto, most commentators have viewed the story of the opera as a realistic one. Yet this fails to account for one other significant point: that Dido does not commit suicide (as she does in Virgil, and again in Marlowe and Nash), nor is there time in the opera for her to pine away from grief before taking her life (as she does in *Brutus of Alba*). This time, the queen is 'invaded' by death as soon as Aeneas has gone. What is more, despite no mention of a weapon or a funeral pyre, the queen dies and Cupids appear over her tomb.

It would seem, then, that Tate was not portraying a realistic tale. But, prompted by the way the British legend had been used over the centuries to comment on the monarchy, it is now easy to pick up what Tate was driving at. Thinking of the two new monarchs on the English throne, he seems to have been pointing out, by means of an allegory, the possible fate of the British nation should Dutch William fail in his responsibilities to his English queen. It is not difficult to imagine the tremendous national upheaval which must have resulted from the deposition of James II. So Tate's choice of subject was apparently intended to reflect the political turbulence that must have been uppermost in many minds in 1689.

THE MISSING MUSIC CONTROVERSY: ANOTHER POINT OF VIEW

GEOFFREY BUSH

~~~~~~~~~~~~~~~

[*A Debate with Benjamin Britten*]†

Benjamin Britten's edition of *Dido and Aeneas* has drawn fire for its over-elaborate and sometimes distracting realization of the basso continuo. But it was not this aspect of the edition to which his compatriot composer and editor Geoffrey Bush objected, rather Britten's decision to supply parodied music for the witches' chorus and dance at the end of the second act. Letters were exchanged in the *Times*, probably the first debate about Purcell to appear on that famous Correspondence Page. In the following excerpt from his memoirs, Bush ruminates on the Fleet Street tempest and self-effacingly reprints all the relevant documents.

By way of an introductory fanfare to the première of his realisation of Purcell's *Dido and Aeneas* at the Lyric Theatre, Hammersmith, on May 1st 1951, Benjamin Britten issued the following statement to the press:

> There is no original manuscript extant of *Dido and Aeneas*—not a note remains in Purcell's handwriting. The oldest manuscript that survives is in the library of St. Michael's College, Tenbury, and is probably early eighteenth century, which contains music to all the opera except for a passage at the end of Act II.
>
> Anyone who has taken part in, or indeed heard, a concert or stage performance, must have been struck by the very peculiar and most unsatisfactory end of this Act II as it stands; Aeneas sings his very beautiful recitative in A minor and disappears without any curtain music or chorus (which occurs in all the other acts). The drama cries out for some strong dramatic music, and the whole key scheme of the opera (very carefully adhered to in each of the other scenes) demands a return to the key of the beginning of the act or its relative major (ie, D [minor], or F major). What is more, the contemporary printed libretto (a copy of which is preserved in the library of The Royal College of Music) has perfectly clear indications for a scene with the Sorceress and her

† From *Left, Right and Centre: Reflections on Composers and Composing* (London: Thames Publishing, 1983), pp. 51-4. Reprinted with permission.

Enchantresses, consisting of six lines of verse, and a dance to end the act. It is my considered opinion that music was certainly composed to this scene and has been lost. It is quite possible that it will be found, but each year makes it less likely.

It is to me of prime importance dramatically as well as musically to include this missing scene, and so I have supplied other music of Purcell's to fit the six lines of the libretto, and a dance to end in the appropriate key. It is interesting in this connection to note that in the 1840 edition published by the Musical Antiquarian Society, it was apparently thought impossible to end the act with a recitative and the difficulty was overcome by including the first two numbers of the next act, *i.e.*, the Sailors' song and dance.

The realization of the figured bass for harpsichord is, of course, my own responsibility; in Purcell's time it was the custom for the keyboard player to work it out afresh at each performance. Therefore, no definitive version of this part is possible or desirable.

By making this pronouncement Britten turned what might have been regarded as a routine occasion into an event distinctly out of the ordinary—a characteristic example of his managerial, as opposed to his musical, genius. All the same, I felt that the statement should not be allowed to pass without comment, if only because—apart from the stated intention to supply some supposedly missing music—it contained no information which had not been generally available for more than half a century.

To the Editor, The Times   [3 May 1951]

Sir, — The peculiar state of the end of Act II of Purcell's opera *Dido and Aeneas* noted by Mr. Benjamin Britten will be familiar to anyone who has studied the Purcell Society's edition published many years ago. It is quite clear from the libretto that Nahum Tate had planned the scene to end with a chorus and dance; it is equally clear from the musical key-scheme that Purcell had intended to fall in with his proposal. What is not clear (and what Mr. Britten does not explain) is how this one short musical section came to be lost when all the rest was carefully preserved. The most probable explanation is that it was deliberately destroyed by the composer himself. When the opera came to actual performance he must have found that Aeneas's solitary and heartbreaking recitatives made a far more effective ending to the act than the conventional witches' chorus previously planned, and the resulting excision was an undoubted stroke of genius. As for Nahum Tate, he seems to have anticipated Sheridan's Mr. Puff: 'To cut out this scene!—but I'll print it—Egad, I'll print it every word.'

The use of the word *carefully*—chosen (ironically enough) not to emphasise a point but to produce a better balanced sentence—proved to be a fatal exaggeration, and my slingshot passed harmlessly over Britten's head.

To the Editor, The Times.

Sir, — In his letter of May 3 Dr Geoffrey Bush states that Purcell's music to *Dido and Aeneas* has been 'carefully preserved'. That is not quite the case. The only surviving manuscript of the music seems to be one written by John Travers 25 years after the death of Purcell and 40 years after the only contemporary performance of the work. Travers was not born at the time of this performance, and judging by obvious copying errors in the manuscript he cannot have been very familiar with the work, and it can never have been used for performance.* The source for Dr W H Cummings's Purcell Society edition was written 'probably in Purcell's time' (Dr Cummings's words). This came to light in the 1880s and has since disappeared (according to Professor E J Dent). It differs widely from the above Travers manuscript which is preserved in the library of St. Michael's College, Tenbury. There was apparently yet another manuscript consulted by Mac-Farren for his edition of the work for the Musical Antiquarian Society in 1841, which again differs from the above version, actually being considerably shorter. It seems that there is no trace of this manuscript to-day. 'Carefully preserved' is, therefore, a scarcely accurate phrase to use.

The musical scheme of *Dido and Aeneas* is remarkable: each scene is a complete unit containing many numbers in closely related keys following each other without pause, and ending in the same tonality or its relative major or minor as it started in (very much like his own verse-anthems and sonatas in fact). That Purcell, as Dr Bush suggests, should suddenly at the last moment abandon this plan for one of the scenes seems to me inconceivable. For one thing, it is completely foreign to the aesthetic attitude of the time. For another, it suggests that he rated the part played by tonality in form as low as many composers do to-day. No, I am afraid that I accept the verdict of the one piece of contemporary evidence we have—the libretto—and judge that the work still remains, alas, incomplete. Until such a happy event as the discovery of the missing numbers occurs, I believe it is better to restore the original symmetry of the work with Purcellian material than to leave this wonderful musical building with a large hole in it.

Had I only known it, the perfect demonstration of the unreliability of a printed libretto as operatic evidence was ready to hand—in Britten's own work. Like Purcell, Britten had himself omitted many passages (and altered others) in the libretto of *Peter Grimes*; and like Nahum Tate, Montagu Slater had later published the original version in full. I owe this information to Eric Crozier, who (as first producer of *Peter Grimes*) was in at the birth of the opera. It would not have been easy to discover it unaided because of Slater's prefatory remarks, which are disingenuous to say the least: 'I have omitted some of the repetitions and inversions required by the music . . . thus the present text is *to all intents and purposes the one to which the music was composed*' (my italics). Leaving aside the many minor alterations and omissions, Slater's text of Peter Grimes' two great monologues (in his hut, Act II scene 2,

*The Tenbury manuscript was not copied by Travers. See Eric Walter White, "New Light on 'Dido and Aeneas'," *Henry Purcell 1659–1695*, ed. Imogen Holst (London, 1959), p. 15. [*Editor.*]

and on the beach, Act III, scene 2) bears little or no relation to what is sung in the opera. I ought, however, to have recalled for myself that Dryden was on record as being obliged to 'cramp his verses' when collaborating with Purcell on their opera *King Arthur*. If Purcell could dictate to a giant like Dryden, how much more ruthlessly would he not have been prepared to treat Nahum Tate, a vastly inferior poet?

Recently the tonal argument has also been destroyed, by Ellen Harris . . . In her book *Handel and the Pastoral Tradition* [the relevant passage is reprinted on pp. 243-52]. She has convincingly demonstrated that the accepted sub-division of *Dido and Aeneas* into three unequal acts is as illogical as it is lopsided; properly considered, the opera falls into two symmetrical halves. On this analysis the hunting scene no longer appears as a self-sufficient entity; it is simply the opening section of the second act and as such does not require a completely circular key-scheme of its own.

Even if it were still felt necessary to return to D minor after the departure of the false Mercury and Aeneas' A minor apostrophe to the gods, Purcell himself provided a delightfully elegant expedient which does away with any necessity for recomposition. For this discovery I am indebted to yet another scholar, my friend and colleague Brian Trowell, King Edward Professor of Music at King's College, London. The hunting scene begins with a little prologue for strings entitled *Ritornelle*; what could be simpler or more suitable than to make it "come round again" at the end in the guise of an epilogue? There need be no fear that repetition would produce an anti-climax; what was originally heard in the context of hope would now be heard in one of despair. In the hands of a master composer, formal recapitulation can so often produce subtly different emotional effects.

After relying so much on the expertise of others, I would like to add a footnote which, in the familiar phrase of Bertie Wooster's manservant, is a little thing of my own. Opera writers throughout the ages — for example, Mozart and da Ponte using *Non più andrai* as part of Don Giovanni's supper music — have always enjoyed an in-joke. It is my belief that Purcell and Tate were doing precisely that during this same hunting scene which we have been discussing. When Aeneas rejoins the ladies to display the trophies of the chase, he boasts of his success in a curiously convoluted manner:

> Behold, upon my bending spear
> A monster's head stands bleeding,
> With tushes far exceeding
> Those that did Venus' huntsmen tear.

On the surface this is simply a nod in the direction of classical mythology; but I would like to think that the *cognoscenti* among Josias Priest's audience were able to translate it and relish the real meaning underneath:

"John Blow's *Venus and Adonis* is dead; long live Henry Purcell's *Dido and Aeneas*!"

ELLEN T. HARRIS

[*The Design of the Tenbury Manuscript*]†

Siding firmly with Geoffrey Bush against Benjamin Britten and others who have detected a gap at the end of Act II of *Dido and Aeneas*, Ellen T. Harris, Professor of Music at the University of Chicago, argues that the Tenbury score is a faithful copy of Purcell's original which lacks nothing except perhaps the prologue. Her argument is complex and provocative, and while it may not silence those who regard the score as an imperfect record of what Purcell wrote, the following analysis questions several basic assumptions about the structure of the opera.

A study of the libretto for *Dido and Aeneas* reveals that Purcell was presented with the same structural elements as his predecessors [Matthew Locke and John Blow]. In this opera-masque, however, the balance of these elements moves even further [towards vocally dominated, continuous drama]. That this can be attributed entirely to Purcell, and not to his librettist Nahum Tate, is immediately evident from a comparison of the libretto with the extant score.

Tate's libretto is divided into three acts with an opening prologue. Phoebus, Venus, Spring, and assorted Nereids, Tritons, Nymphs, and Shepherds, Shepherdesses, and Country Maids populate this short prologue. . . . It sets up the nature and actions of the gods who will determine the crisis of the plot. Thus, after one of the Nereids spies Venus rising from the sea, Phoebus speaks to the Nereid about her:

† From *Handel and the Pastoral Tradition* (London: Oxford University Press, 1980), pp. 129–136; 138–140. © 1980 Ellen Harris. Reprinted by permission.

> Whose lustre does out-shine
> Your fainter beams, and half eclipses mine,
> Give *Phoebus* leave to prophesy.
> Phoebus all events can see.
> Ten thousand harmes,
> From such prevailing charmes,
> To Gods and men must instantly ensue (11. 14–20)

The prologue also bows in the direction of Josias Priest, a dancing-master, for whose boarding-school girls this piece was adapted. Into a mere eighty-one lines are incorporated directions for six dances and one instrumental interlude.*

The three acts of the main body of the work are also dance-oriented. Each act ends with a large dance. In Act II, which the libretto divides into two scenes, each scene ends with a dance. Indications for further, specific dances are given throughout: in Act I, 'the Baske' and 'A dance gittars chacony'; in Act II, i, 'Enter 2 Drunken Saylors, a Dance'; in Act II, ii, 'Gitter Ground a Dance', and 'A dance to Entertain Aeneas'; and in Act III, 'The Saylors Dance', and 'Jack of the Lanthorn Leads the Spaniards Out of Their Way Among the Inchanteresses. A Dance.' As opposed to the previous substantive masques, the remaining musical parts of *Dido*, the choruses and solos, are given no strict dramatic shape beyond having choruses precede the four concluding dances. Their words comment on the action and prepare for the ballet.

The primary manuscript score preserved in the Library of St. Michael's College, Tenbury Wells, contains a number of important discrepancies from the extant libretto.[1] The entire Prologue is lacking. Of eleven dances specifically called for in the three main acts, four are set. Some of the omissions are striking. As in Blow's *Venus and Adonis*, there is no final dance. Moreover, all the dances in Tate's first act are lacking but the concluding Triumphing Dance. Also the dance of the drunken sailors, which interrupts the scene of the witches (II, i) in the manner of an antimasque, is deleted, leaving in this scene only the witches' concluding Echo Dance. Missing as well are three dances in Act II, ii. The second act ends with the arioso of Aeneas, omitting also, therefore, the final chorus.

It has become common practice in discussions and editions of *Dido and Aeneas*, indeed it has almost become a competitive sport, to see who can come

---

*See libretto above, pp. 63–66.

1. The Oki Ms., preserved at the Nanki Music Library, is apparently a later source and includes only minor variants. See Imogen Holst, 'A Note on the Nanki Collection of Purcell's Works', in *Henry Purcell (1659–1695): Essays on his Music*, ed. by Imogen Holst (London: Oxford University Press, 1959), pp. 127–30.

up with the most 'complete' score by replacing the 'missing' material with compositions either newly composed or parodied from Purcell's other oeuvre. 'With such a brief piece as *Dido*, the common question in opera of "what can we cut?" becomes for once "what shall we add?" '[2] This situation has arisen because of the unquestioned assumption that the extant music in the Tenbury manuscript is not complete. Indeed, the Tenbury manuscript can be dated no earlier than the second half of the eighteenth century; it is thought to represent a truncated and cut-up version of the opera which was inserted into various stage dramas of 1700 in piecemeal fashion. Thus Tate's libretto has been taken to stand as an authoritative guide to the true score of 1689. However, there are reasons to question these commonly-held beliefs.

First of all, the presumed date of the Tenbury manuscript, the earliest manuscript source, is so much later than even the theatrical representations of *Dido and Aeneas* that there is no reason to believe it associated with them rather than with Purcell's original score. Second, the additional lines set to music (perhaps by Daniel Purcell)[3] in the theatrical versions are at least as conspicuously lacking in the surviving manuscript score as those assumed to be missing according to Tate's libretto. Third, although the distribution of scenes in the manuscript does not correspond to Tate's libretto, it relates even less to that of the later representations where the second and third scenes were not simply labelled differently but actually reversed.[4] Finally, there are many differences between Tate's libretto and the surviving musical sources besides the obvious omissions. These seem designed, and all have been taken unquestioningly, or at least without comment, to represent Purcell's improvement of the libretto. It is not immediately clear why other changes and omissions could not derive from Purcell as well as these.

For example, it is clearly Purcell who makes Belinda into a chorus leader.[5] Where Tate writes (in Act I) a separate and completely rounded-off lyric for Belinda followed by a choral couplet:

> *Bel.* Shake the cloud from off your brow,
> Fate your wishes do allow.
> Empire growing,
> Pleasures flowing,
> Fortune smiles and so should you,
> Shake the cloud from off your brow,

---

2. Roger Savage, see below, pp. 256–57.

3. Eric Walter White, 'New Light on *Dido and Aeneas*,' pp. 50–2 [but see above, p. 17].

4. In Tate's libretto the second and third scenes are labelled Act II, i and ii. In the manuscript score they are labelled Act I, ii, and Act II. See below, p. 247. In the theatrical representations they have no corresponding labels but appear in reverse order.

5. This appellation derives from Dent, p. 188 [quoted above, p. 215].

> *Cho.*   Banish sorrow, banish care,
>   Grief should ne'er approach the fair.

Purcell fuses the two together into one number, the chorus's music growing logically out of Belinda's music and completing it.

Often Belinda's part grows on account of Purcell's conception of it. In Act I, Tate writes:

> *Bel.*   Grief encreasing, by concealing
>
> *Dido.*   Mine admits of no revealing.
>
> *Bel.*   Then let me speak the Trojan guest,
>   Into your tender thoughts has prest.
>
> *2 women.*   The greatest blessing fate can give.
>   Our *Carthage* to secure, and *Troy* revive.

Purcell sets this as dialogue in recitative between the hesitant Queen and her encouraging, forthright handmaiden. Belinda acquires the lines of the '2 women', increasing the personal and dramatic intensity of the situation.

There exist in the score several similar examples.

1. In the recitative: 'Whence could so much virtue', Belinda alone responds to her mistress where Tate gives some of the lines to '2 women'.

2. In the solo-chorus, 'Fear no danger', Tate writes one line for Belinda, one for the '2 women' and four for the chorus. Purcell sets all six lines as a duet between Belinda and one other woman (later called the attendant), then repeats the entire piece for chorus.

3. In the solo-chorus: 'Thanks to these lovesome vales', Tate gives Belinda one line, the chorus three. Purcell has Belinda sing all the four followed by a repetition for the chorus.

4. In Tate's libretto (Act II, ii), Dido sings,

> The skies are clouded, heark how thunder
> Rends the mountain oaks asunder,
> Hast, hast, to town this open field,
> No shelter from the storm can yield.

Purcell gives Dido the first two lines, preceded by a short recitative for Aeneas. Then Belinda sings the next two, as usual leading in the full chorus. This creates a particularly pleasing dramatic effect with the entire hunting party urging one another off the stage.

Belinda becomes in Purcell's hands the spokeswoman for the townspeople who, initially dumb, respond enthusiastically to all she says. A similar effect is made in the separate scenes for the witches and for the sailors. Purcell creates, respectively, a first and second witch and a first sailor. These accepted textual alterations of *Dido and Aeneas* suggest a closer look at other differences between the libretto and score is necessary.

Of the so-called missing dances, at least two may only be hidden. 'The Baske' in Act I may well have been performed to the chorus, 'Fear no danger'. The use of a danced chorus would hardly be an innovation. In addition, the long instrumental postlude to the attendant's aria in Act II, ii, may have been used for the dance 'to entertain Aeneas'. However, it is the missing chorus at the conclusion of Tate's Act II that represents the thorniest problem for Purcell's would-be revisers; there are now at least three 'solutions' available to modern performers.[6] The felt necessity for these appears to neglect important internal evidence. For example, there is a musical parallel between the concluding arioso of Aeneas and Dido's Lament at the conclusion of the following act. At the moments of their greatest stress, in each case resultant from their imminent separation, both characters break into non-literate vocalizations.

The settings are identical, emphasizing the structural importance of the two laments. Although it seems never to have been thought possible that the scenic divisions in the manuscript score might represent an authentic version, it is necessary to look again at the implications of these.

Where Tate writes three well-balanced acts, the second in two scenes, the manuscript score contains three acts of widely varying lengths created by the placement of two scenes in Act I.

Tate	Tenbury Ms.
Act I	Act I, i
Act II, i	Act I, ii
Act II, ii	Act II
Act III	Act III

6. The Boosey and Hawkes edition by Britten and Holst and the Purcell Society (Novello) edition by Dart and Laurie both make use of other music by Purcell to which they fit Tate's text as a contrafactus. In Savage, 'Producing *Dido and Aeneas*,' pp. 405-6, Michael Tilmouth offers a newly-composed finale [reprinted above, pp. 183-187].

Thus the manuscript's first act is approximately half again the size of Tate's. The second act is less than half as long since the final chorus and ballet are omitted as well. * * * A graphic presentation of these differences is:

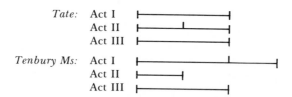

Dent mentions the alteration of the first two acts and concludes that 'the difference is of no importance'.[7] But the symmetry of the opera is apparently ruined. A closer examination reveals that the layout of the manuscript may not be as unimportant as has generally been thought.

The larger musical structure of the score implies not three major sections, as in the libretto, but two of equal length. With minor differences these exhibit a very similar plan.[8]

TABLE 1

Dramatic Structure of *Dido and Aeneas*

Part I:	I Ç S r Ç r	Ç r C r S C D	[pr] C[rCrC] S C D
Part II:	I Ç [Sp] r Ç r	[pÇ] D r S C D	r C r S C

I:	separate instrumental piece
Ç:	chorus with solo introductions
C:	chorus
D:	dance
S:	solo
r:	recitative
p:	instrumental postlude or prelude attached to another piece
[ ]:	a unit made up of multiple parts.

7. Dent, *Foundations*, p. 180.

8. There are three divisions in each section. With the sections indicated by Roman numeral and the divisions by letter, the divisions in the libretto (L) and score (S) are as follows:

Part:	IA	1B	IC	IIA	IIB	IIC
L:	I		II, i	II, ii	III	
S:	I, i		I, ii	II	III	

This visual layout brings into relief certain other facets of the surviving musical sources. There are only two independent instrumental symphonies — one at the beginning of each major section. At more minor divisions (the beginnings of Tate's Act II and III), an instrumental prelude is substituted. In the layout of the two parallel sections conflicting musical types coincide only once — a chorus with a dance in the second sections. One does not interpret this lack of symmetry as a major breach, however, and it may well explain why there survives only one setting of an intermediate dance movement.

The musical group [rCrC] in the last division of the first part parallels the recitative in the second part since the choral sections consist simply of interruptive laughter. They are not independent; the music is continuous. In another recitative (after the dance in the second division of the second part) laughing is similarly incorporated in smaller patches. Finally, the omission, at the end of Tate's second act, of the chorus and dance can be attributed as much to a desire for symmetry as to a dramatic urge to end with Aeneas's despair; and the musical relationship between this recitative and Dido's Lament ties together the dramatic thrust of Part II after which follows the Grand Choral Finale to the entire opera.

Each large section is divided into three parts. In two cases these divisions are marked by act or scene changes to a new locale. Moreover, each section has its own tonal centre. The introduction of Dido, which depicts her hesitation to submit to her feelings is written in C minor (section 1). The key changes to C major for the optimism of Belinda *et al.*, the entrance of Aeneas, and the triumph of emotion over both reason and destiny (section 2). The resolution of the witches to destroy this new-found happiness evolves in the tonal centre of F major (section 3). The hunt (section 4) emphasizes D minor/D major. When the sailors prepare to depart, and the witches see their success (section 5), the centre moves to B♭ major. Finally, Dido's anguish and death (section 6) conclude the opera in G minor.

Assuming that the score (but not the libretto) was planned in two large and parallel sections, each one includes three dramatic and tonal divisions. Dramatically the six sections form a perfect arch.

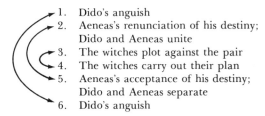

      1. Dido's anguish
      2. Aeneas's renunciation of his destiny;
         Dido and Aeneas unite
      3. The witches plot against the pair
      4. The witches carry out their plan
      5. Aeneas's acceptance of his destiny;
         Dido and Aeneas separate
      6. Dido's anguish

Harmonically the first three sections move from the key of the minor dominant to the major dominant to the major tonic in the key of F. The second
three sections follow the same progression, with the interpolation of a major-
mediant section, in the key of G minor. Thus instead of having each section in
one key as does Locke, or making rather primitive efforts at connecting separate tonal sections, as does Blow, Purcell writes two sections in independent
tonic areas with parallel and logical harmonic progressions. Benjamin Britten's
argument that the 'second act' is proven incomplete because the tonality demands a return to the key of the beginning of the act (D minor) or its parallel
major not only depends on an implicit trust in Tate's act divisions but on a
tonal scheme in advance of Purcell's music [see above, pp. 239-41].

The care with which Purcell put this work together is astonishing.
Equally astonishing is Dent's comment: '[*Dido and Aeneas*] conforms to no
tradition; it has no sense of style; but it is saved from falling into the merely
picturesque by its robust directness.'[9] The opera is clearly based on the
masque tradition and grows quite naturally out of works by Lawes, Locke,
and Blow. Blow had already brought about an important re-orientation in
the form; Purcell, Blow's student, continued in that direction. Both deprive
the dance of its primary position. As opposed to the often unconnected entrées
of the *ballet de Cour* and the popularity of a parallel antimasque tradition in
England, one witnesses a new trend toward dramatic unity. The movement
from the five entrées in Locke's *Cupid and Death* to the three acts and a prologue in *Venus and Adonis* to the two large musical sections in *Dido and
Aeneas*, is one obvious result of this trend. The growing harmonic sophistica-
tion in the scores of Locke, Blow, and Purcell further reflects it. Locke emphasizes each of his sections with distinct and unrelated tonal centres. Blow
attempts to relate the sections with hasty modulations at their beginnings or
ends. Still, however, there exists no overall harmonic direction. Purcell, like
Locke, emphasizes his sectionalization with distinct tonal centres. Each section, however, is not static but includes direct harmonic motion toward its
own tonic. Purcell's division of the score into halves also serves to emphasize
the arch form of the drama, a complete renunciation of the episodic plot.

*   *   *

The accepted position that the Tenbury manuscript preserves *Dido and
Aeneas* in an incomplete form is based on the presumption that it was copied
from the score used in the 1704 representations of the opera. The argument is

9. Dent, *Foundations*, p. 188.

as follows. In the theatrical productions of 1700, when sections of the opera were inserted into a play, the two scenes of Tate's Act II were reversed, perhaps in order to conclude with a magical incantation scene.[10] Furthermore, the scene now first (Tate's II, ii) was augmented after Aeneas' recitative to include a discussion about the opposing forces of Love and Honour between Aeneas and two of his friends. This was followed as in Tate's libretto by the entrance of the witches and a concluding chorus and dance. The prologue was inserted last and altered so that it ends not with pastoral material but with a newly written duet between Mars and Peace. 'This provides a much stronger ending, in the classical as opposed to the pastoral vein.'[11] In fact, all of the alterations in *Dido* for its appearance as a dramatic opera in 1700 seem designed to give it the heroic qualities lacking in the original and thought more appropriate to the English operatic genre.

In its use as an afterpiece in 1704, these changes were dropped, and the opera reverted to a form 'approximating' the original. The scenes of Tate's second act were repositioned correctly, but presumably mislabelled in such a way that Act II, i, still ended an act, although now Act I, and Act II, ii, still began an act. The added material in Act II, ii, was omitted, as was the entire prologue in any form. The assumption seems to be that in dropping the added material, the original ending of the scene, purportedly still included in 1700, was also dropped. This, as stated above, is the most troublesome problem for modern editors of *Dido and Aeneas*, all of whom assume that the production of 1689 did include the numbers at the end of Act II. No one, however, has stated clearly whether these numbers were included in 1704. The reasoning seems to be that since the Tenbury manuscript is based on that performance and does not include those numbers, then they were not performed in 1704. However, the 'omission' of the numbers from the end of Act II seems to be the reason for assuming that the Tenbury manuscript represents the 1704 productions, making the arguments tautological. Indeed, there seems no reason whatsoever to assume that the productions of *Dido and Aeneas* in 1704 differed in any appreciable way from the original. It seems doubly odd to argue that the 1704 productions represent Purcell's intentions except for the end of this one scene when there are so many other textual variants from Tate's libretto as well.

Contrary to common opinion, then, there is sufficient reason to assume that the score of *Dido and Aeneas* as it has been preserved, except perhaps for the missing Prologue, reflects Purcell's original intentions. Even the manu-

---

10. White, 'New Light', pp. 23–4.
11. Ibid., p. 28.

script evidence can be seen to point in that direction. Eric Walter White says of the Tenbury score, 'not only it is clean and clear, but internal evidence shows it was based on a very early score—possibly Purcell's own original manuscript as adapted for use in the theatre. The style of notation and the restricted use of figuration imply that the original must date from the end of the seventeenth or beginning of the eighteenth century.'[12] White thus seems to leave open the possibility that the source for the Tenbury manuscript copy could predate the theatrical revivals of 1700 and 1704. When he discusses the absence of the 1700 additions, however, he holds on to the view that they were *deleted*, either by the Tenbury scribe or at some prior time. Apparently because of the missing numbers at the end of Tate's Act II, White rejects the possibility that the source from which the scribe copied represented a version previous to the additions of 1700.

> The extra music that was used in *The Loves of Dido and Aeneas* in 1700 does not appear to have survived. It is even doubtful whether it was carried over into the 1704 revivals, for there is no trace of any consciousness on the part of the Tenbury MS scribe that there were omissions in the score from which he was copying. It is always possible that this extra music may turn up; but the likelihood now seems rather remote.[13]

And White's conclusions adhere to the traditional view, connecting by default the added music of 1700 with the numbers at the end of Tate's Act II.

> Meanwhile, any modern edition of the opera (such as Britten's) that attempts to fill the gaps in the score as it has come down to us with appropriate music by Purcell is to be welcomed as a step towards the fuller realization of the true nature of the operatic masterpiece that Tate and Purcell planned and created together.[14]

The analysis given here, dividing *Dido and Aeneas* into two equal parts, highlights some of the problems inherent in the traditional view of Purcell's opera as incomplete. It also emphasizes the fact that the difficulty in dating the surviving sources hinges not on these manuscripts themselves but on the lost sources from which they were copied. Until clearer evidence is found, however, it seems most unlikely that the symmetry apparent in this two-part division could be the accidental result of mutilations made more than a decade after Purcell composed his original score for *Dido and Aeneas*.

12. White, 'New Light', p. 15.
13. Ibid., p. 34.
14. Ibid.

PRODUCTION AND
INTERPRETATION

ROGER SAVAGE

Producing Dido and Aeneas[†]

Roger Savage, a member of the Department of English at the University of Edinburgh, is a noted drama and opera critic. And he speaks from experience — as a
director whose productions of baroque opera, while striving for historical accu-
racy, have been perfectly at home in the modern theater.

Mounting any opera presents a number of problems. Mounting pre-Mozartian
opera doubles the number. When the producer and conductor have agreed
about the casting, pacing and general feel of the piece, the conductor must
wrestle with all sorts of issues: vocal/instrumental timbre and balance, continuo realization, tempi, decoration, double dots and so on. And the producer
has not only to face the normal challenges of his craft: achieving a good rap-
port with his designer and choreographer; sensitizing his singers to dramatic
values; devising a chain of stage-images which seemingly provoke the words of
the libretto and the notes of the music; establishing a rate of eventuation in
stage-business which complements the time-scale of the score. With opera
before the 1780s he has also to solve problems created by the lapse or loss over
the last two centuries of performance conventions, audience expectations,
areas of shared knowledge, sometimes even of crucial documents. The sixteen
paragraphs which follow are one producer's account of the problems of this
sort raised by Purcell's *Dido and Aeneas*. Some of them are typical, others less
so; but in this case the untypical ones are not unimportant. They arise from
the opera's almost certainly having been commissioned for and premiered by
largely amateur forces ("Perform'd at Mr. Josias Priest's Boarding-School at
Chelsey. By Young Gentlewomen" as the 1689 libretto has it) in an England
unused to continuously sung music-drama. The result was a piece fairly sim-

† Reprinted, with revisions by the author, from *Early Music*, 4 (1976), 393–406, by permission of the Editor and Oxford University Press. © Oxford University Press.

ple to perform adequately, barely an hour long, and well-nigh dominated by its chorus. These things, together with its superb musical quality, have led to *Dido* becoming very popular since the turn of this century, especially with amateurs. Hence it has to be well, and not just adequately, done, and here its highly-charged brevity makes life very difficult from the staging point of view. Once the curtain is up there is no time to waste and no room for by-play. Each tableau, step, gesture, prop and lighting-cue must arise from necessity and have its effect at once, and yet there must be no point-making which draws attention to itself and so distracts from the depth and flow of the music. *Dido* is in fact a tall order for a producer. Schoenberg on Webern comes to mind: it is easy enough to turn a sigh into a novel, less so to convey a novel in a sigh.

1. HOW DOES ONE PROGRAMME *DIDO*?

With only sixty minutes' worth of music and no real opportunity for an interval, *Dido and Aeneas* needs to be paired with another work to make an evening. There are several possibilities:

(i) *The Original Prologue:* a masque-like piece for which the libretto but no music survives. Reconstructions using music from elsewhere in Purcell are possible, however, and one has been published by Thurston Dart and Margaret Laurie in their edition (London: Novello, 1961, rev. 1966), though even this would not very much increase the length of the evening, being twenty minutes long at most.

(ii) *A Curtain-Raiser:* something perhaps of roughly the same age and mood as *Dido* and calling for similar resources, e.g. the *Ballo delle Ingrate* or *Combattimento di Tancredi e Clorinda* of Monteverdi, or Act I of Cavalli's *La Didone* (a *Prise de Troie* to go with Purcell's *Troyens à Carthage*), or Marc-Antoine Charpentier's "opéra de chasse," *Actéon*, which has the same physical setting as the Grove scene in *Dido* ("Here Actaeon met his fate . . .").

(iii) *An Afterpiece:* a short, light work from roughly the same period as *Dido* with some connection (perhaps parodic) in subject or treatment, such as Lampe's *Dragon of Wantley*; or — if money allows — a contrasting work which overlaps *Dido* in some way, e.g. Weill's *Seven Deadly Sins*, which also presents a woman's destruction by worldly experience and also juxtaposes song and dance.

(iv) *A Modern Complement:* the one-act opera *Fanny Robin* written by Edward Harper specifically as a companion-piece for *Dido*, which it quotes, parallels and consciously differs from in various ways, notably by using the English ballad-motif of the Soldier Who Rode Away rather than the classical epic one. Harper's opera (Oxford University Press, 1979) calls for a profes-

Late 17th-century costume
design in the manner of
Jean Bérain

sional in the lead but can otherwise be managed by amateur forces. (Though based on Thomas Hardy's *Far from the Madding Crowd* and quoting English folk-song, its musical idiom is very much of the 1970s.)

2. IS THERE A RELIABLE PERFORMING EDITION OF THE OPERA?

If that means a definitive edition, the answer is no, since no autograph score or contemporary printing of the music is known to survive, only the printed libretti from 1689 and 1700 which do not always agree with each other and which depart in various ways from a group of 18th-century manuscript copies of the original score which quite often differ among themselves. Still, each of the editions of the work now available — Dent's for Oxford University Press, Britten and Holst's for Boosey and Hawkes, and Laurie/Dart's for Novello (which first saw the light of day as a performing edition by both of them in 1961 and later became the Purcell Society scholarly edition by Laurie reprinted in the present volume) — is responsible and respectable; and it is worth the producer's while to establish all his options among the surviving music, words and stage directions by looking at all of them carefully. It is best to look at the miniature score rather than the vocal score in the case of Britten/Holst, but to look at both Novello scores, since they complement each other. Do not feel that as producer you have to leave all such matters to your conductor. (For instance, from a producer's point of view there is much to be said for the Oki manuscript's variant setting of the words "Our next motion/Must be to storm . . ." in the Sorceress's last aria, as given in the appendix to Britten/Holst; and I prefer the 1689 libretto's "Let Jove say what he will" in Aeneas's last recitative to the various manuscripts' limp-wristed "say what he please.") With such a brief piece as *Dido*, the common question in opera of "what can we cut?" becomes for once "what can we add?" The answer depends on what one takes to be the relation between the score as it survives and the surviving libretti. To Dent's edition one must almost certainly add witching music for the end of the Grove scene ("Then since our charms have sped . . .") and possibly the two guitar dances that the 1689 libretto mentions; to Britten/Holst (which has witches' music for "Since our charms" arranged from other Purcell works) one may want to add the guitar dances; while the Laurie/Dart 1961 performing edition is pretty well "complete," though its guitar numbers in the appendix are only bases for improvisation and its continuo realization throughout is—for better or worse—not as striking as Dent's or Britten's. However, be warned: some of the end-of-Grove-scene music which is supplied in Britten/Holst has the disadvantage of now being perhaps too well known from its original context in *The Indian Queen*, while the Laurie/Dart solution to the problem at this point, though also using "real" Purcell, is somewhat untheatrical in that it allows the poor witches no time to get on stage before flinging them into solid four-part harmony. A different, and I think very effective solution is printed on pp. 183–87 of this volume: a piece of unashamed pastiche by Professor Michael Tilmouth of the Purcell Society.

3. IS THERE ANYTHING GOOD TO READ BEFORE REHEARSALS BEGIN?

Perhaps the three best things from Purcell's own age are a 17th-century English version of Book IV of Vergil's *Aeneid* (the most thorough classical treatment of the Dido myth), Sir William Davenant's Restoration adaptation of *Macbeth* (first printed in 1674 and almost certainly the source of the opera's witches), and Nahum Tate's *Brutus of Alba, or the Enchanted Lovers* (1678), a tragedy loosely based on the Dido myth by Purcell's future librettist. The outstanding Vergil version is Dryden's, which first appeared in 1697 and is to be found in all good editions of his poems. This has a fine Restoration-classical flavor, and it is immaterial that it postdates *Dido and Aeneas*, since (as far as I know) Tate did not make use of any specific translation while writing his text. (His reliance on the Latin original, on the other hand, is often marked. For instance, Dido's odd rhetorical question about Aeneas in the first scene—

"What battles did he sing?"—is not so much a suggestion that characters in tragical operas never merely *speak* as a translation of *Aeneid* IV.14: *"quae bella exhausta canebat"*; and Aeneas's "What language can I try/My injured queen to pacify?" in the Grove scene is very close to Vergil at IV. 283-4.) Davenant's *Macbeth* version appears in Christopher Spencer's admirable *Five Restoration Adaptations of Shakespeare* (1965), but *Brutus of Alba* will only be found in big learned libraries, which is no loss to the rest of the world considering its general awfulness, interesting though it is for its formidable Sorceress and its hints of appropriate business and decor for *Dido*. As for preparatory reading from the last sixty years, apart from the other essays included in the present Critical Score, the most worthwhile things are, I think, Eric Walter White's scholarly essay, "New Light on *Dido and Aeneas*," in *Henry Purcell 1659-1695* (a tercentenary *Festschrift* edited in 1959 by Imogen Holst), and Graham Sheffield's survey of the recordings of *Dido* in *Opera on Record 2* (ed. Alan Blyth, 1983). Elsewhere there are insights to be had from Selma Cohen's account of *Dido's* godfather and probable choreographer Josias Priest in her essay on Restoration theatrical dancing in the *Bulletin of the New York Public Library*, 63 (1959), and from Dennis Arundell's contention that *Dido* was premiered in the open air—see Chapter XII of his *The Critic at the Opera* (1957). Finally there is a just and lively defense of Tate as librettist by Imogen Holst in her collection mentioned above, still perhaps necessary to counter his die-hard reputation as a comical incompetent. (I myself believe that his libretto has only one real lapse, which is that Dido's important sentence beginning "Mean wretches' grief can touch . . ." in the opening scene is syntactically too obscure for singing. Equally there is, I think, only one solecism in Purcell's setting: Dido's crucial phrase "To death I'll fly" in her quarrel with Aeneas is set in such a way that it is normally inaudible. The other moment of obscurity in most performances, and it needs strong production to clarify it, is the Sorceress's sentence beginning, "But when they've done, my trusty elf . . . ," where perhaps Tate and Purcell should share the blame.)

4. HOW FAR SHOULD A PRODUCTION EXPLOIT THE CONNECTION WITH VERGIL'S *AENEID*?

Here a little learning is a dangerous thing. It tempts us to rap Purcell and Tate over the knuckles for "getting Vergil wrong" and set out to correct them in production. This is counterproductive, however. Certainly any intelligent member of the audience at the premiere would have seen *Dido and Aeneas* as a creative interpretation, a reworking of episodes in the *Aeneid*, not as a simple setting of Vergil. And this was quite acceptable Baroque practice:

In our deep vaulted cell the charm we'll prepare:
Too dreadful a practice for this open air.

Giacomo Torelli's setting for the prologue to Corneille's *Andromède* (Paris, 1650)

Busenello was just as cavalier with Vergil in his text for Cavalli's *La Didone* in 1641, and so was Metastasio in his *Didone Abbandonata* libretto, first set by Domenico Sarro in 1724 and all the rage for some years afterwards. What Tate and Purcell do is to leave out all references to Aeneas's son and Dido's former husband, turn her sister Anna into a warm-hearted but rather flighty confidante called Belinda, consummate the lovers' passion well before the celebrated storm and not during it, have Aeneas dispatched from Carthage by an evil trick rather than the will of Rome-creating providence, and suggest that Dido simply dies of a broken heart without wild cries of revenge and the need for a funeral pyre. As if this were not enough, they allow Aeneas a final (though rejected) surrender to love rather than duty, and give a third or so of their opera to the Iago-like plottings of a coven of Gothic spirits who have no original in Vergil at all (where the malign Juno of the *Aeneid* would certainly disown them) and who derive pretty clearly from the Davenant *Macbeth* which superseded Shakespeare's in the Restoration and for which (coincidentally or not) Josias Priest devised the dances. (Put a few lines of Davenant's additions to Shakespeare—

> At the night-Raven's dismal voice,
> Whilst others tremble, we rejoyce;
> And nimbly, nimbly dance we still
> To th'Ecchoes from an hollow Hill . . .
> Let's to the Cave and our dire Charms prepare

—beside Tate's Cave scene in *Dido* and you will see what I mean.) What is
more, Tate and Purcell are clearly much more interested in Dido than in the
Trojan hero. Indeed, it might have saved a lot of misunderstanding if they
had called their opera *The Tragedy of Dido Queen of Carthage*, as Marlowe
did his play a century before. But none of this is to imply that their work is
anything other than quite consistent in itself. It is simply to suggest that, in
our age of classical illiteracy, a producer should call on Vergil only with a lot
of circumspection, except of course where the poet can help to explain small
obscurities in the libretto such as the reference in the first scene to that "tale
so strong" sung offstage by Aeneas. (The listeners needed to be strong too,
since the tale consisted of the equivalent of the 1500 hexameters which make
up Books II and III of the *Aeneid*.) Tate and Purcell are really writing an
opera on Dido and *fate*, a word which appears no less than ten times in the
libretto, and using *what* they please *how* they please from the *Aeneid, Macbeth* and so on.

5. IS THERE A PROPER DECOR FOR THE OPERA?

I can see no reason for setting the opera in a Trojan-Punic world either of
neo-classical imagination or of accurate archaeology. There might be room
for both in a decor for the *Trojans* of Berlioz (which, incidentally, is much
more straightforwardly Vergilian, and in places Shakespearean, than *Dido*);
but both would be anachronistic to a tragedy of 1689, neo-classicism by a 100
years and "correct historical detail" by about 150. Edward Gordon Craig
wrote in the programme for the epoch-making production of *Dido* he designed and produced in 1900 that he had "taken particular care to be entirely
incorrect in all matters of detail"; and Craig is often a good example to follow.
After all, the opera is essentially a study of the conflicting emotions of an
archetypal woman of social and psychological stature. It could be argued in
fact that, leaving aside Aeneas and his *buffo* counterpart the tenor-solo sailor,
all the characters in the opera are really personified aspects *of* Dido: Belinda
and the Second Woman projections of her yearning towards erotic fulfillment, the Sorceress a formidable anti-self embodying all her insecurities and
apprehensions of disaster contingent on her involving herself in any deep personal relationship, and the two solo witches nightmarish shadows of Belinda
and the Second Woman. If this is so, it is tempting and perhaps desirable to
set the opera now—as one might set a similar Baroque psycho-tragedy dominated by one woman, Racine's *Phèdre* (1677)—in a post-naturalistic *lieu
vague* created purely by light, with abstract costumes and symbolic props (cf.
that memorable modernistic line from Guillaume de Vere-Tipple's *Aeneas on
the Saxophone*:

> And Dido on her lilo à sa proie attachée

See, Madam, where the prince appears!
Such sorrow in his looks he bears
As would convince you still he's true.

Part of Antoine Watteau's painting *Les Comédiens Français* of about 1720

as preserved for us by Osbert Lancaster in *Drayneflete Revealed . . .*). This was something of Craig's approach in the 1900 production: a poetic exploitation of colored light and sheer space which is vividly described in Edward Craig's life of his father (1968) and in Denis Bablet's monograph on him (translated into English in 1966). Far better this, certainly, than designing *Dido* as a chunk of Carthaginian history. Better still though, I feel, to set it *à l'antique* in the 17th-century sense, with flats and shutters representing grand vistas which change by unseen hands from colonnades to cliffs to trees in full view of the audience (not as expensive to rig up as they might sound), with flamboyant Roman-Baroque tragic costumes for hero and heroine (cuirasses, plumes and such) and perhaps a flying "machine" to allow the false Mercury and drooping Cupids to descend properly. (The Cupids are cousins to those in Shadwell's *Psyche* of 1675, the decor for which is discussed in the Restoration chapter of Sybil Rosenfeld's *Short History of Scene Design in Great Britain*, 1973.) Again, one could derive the costumes for the witches from the *Macbeth* engraving in Nicholas Rowe's early 18th-century edition of Shakespeare. For the designer to do all this is no more "merely antiquarian" than for the musical director to use a harpsichord as a continuo instrument or a counter-tenor for his false Mercury. Besides, it provides a visual style which complements the musical-verbal style and so helps the audience to focus with the necessary speed on the real issues of the opera: passion, duty and the human condition (or "Cupid," "empire" and "fate," to use Tate's language).

6. SHOULD THERE BE A DOUBLE CHORUS?

What little we know about the first performance of *Dido* suggests something fairly modest in the way of decor and casting; and it was presumably the large number of fairly talented amateur singers available at Mr. Priest's boarding-school which led to the remarkable dominance of the chorus in the opera. (It has as many bars to sing as Dido, Aeneas and the Sorceress put together.) However, speculation can point both ways when it comes to considering whether Purcell intended there to be one chorus-group playing Dido's courtiers and another the witches and sailors, or whether he expected the same group to play all the choral parts. Certainly if there is enough singing talent and costume cash available, the two-group arrangement is easier on the wardrobe-mistress and stage-manager, since it cuts out a series of frantic back-stage costume changes; yet I am not sure that it is really preferable. The easy-going sensuality of Dido's court and the bitchiness of the witches are equally inimical to the queen's happiness, and this comes over very clearly if it is evident to an audience that the same troupe of talented masqueraders is playing both. There is a corollary to this which is on the face of it absurd, that the same singer should play both Dido and the Sorceress. But even here the absurdity would be one of over-emphasis rather than perversity. And is it *so* absurd? Janet Baker has played the Sorceress in the Banquetting Hall at Hampton Court and Dido in the Baroque theatre at Drottningholm. Could someone not be prevailed on to play both in the same production, Odette/Odile-fashion?

7. THE EVIL SISTERS: ARE THEY COMIC OR SINISTER?

The Sorceress, her two attendants and the ho-hoing chorus do not take part in a detachable sub-plot of light relief. They are essential to the idea-pattern of the opera in that they embody the Spirit That Denies and justify, or perhaps represent, the heroine's insecurity. Also they are essential to the intrigue in that it is they who create the false Mercury who tricks Aeneas into leaving Dido. The divergence from Vergil here is especially significant. Vergil's heroic

Wayward sisters! you that fright
The lonely traveller by night . . .

Louis du Guernier's frontispiece
for *Macbeth* in Rowe's second
edition of Shakespeare's works,
1714

Aeneas needs to be rescued by the good gods from his Carthaginian enchant-ress because she is, among other things, a Circe-figure and the embodiment of Rome's traditional enemy across the Mediterranean. Granted, Tate and Pur-cell's Aeneas is also destined to found Rome; but it is a coven of evil sisters who maliciously set the founding of Rome in direct opposition to continuing a love affair with a never-less-than-sympathetic Dido; and it is they, not Jove, who contrive to have the affair snapped off the first night after its consumma-tion. This is behavior worthy of their close relations, Shakespeare's Weird Sis-ters. (The Sorceress in *Dido* even "quotes" *Macbeth*—I.iii.32, I.v.8 or II.i.20 —with her very first words by calling up her "wayward sisters," this being the phrase used in all 17th-century texts of Shakespeare and Shakespeare/ Davenant: it was later editors who changed the adjective to "weird.") The

motiveless malignity of *Macbeth*'s hags relates them to Iago in *Othello*, and
Iago's aside at the climax of Othello and Desdemona's happiness —

> O, you are well tuned now!
> But I'll set down the pegs that make this music

— anticipates the Sorceress's

> The Queen of Carthage, whom we hate,
> As we do all in prosperous state,
> Ere sunset shall most wretched prove,
> Deprived of fame, of life and love

just as her coven's "Destruction's our delight,/Delight our greatest sorrow" is
anticipated by the "Fair is foul, and foul is fair" of the *Macbeth* witches. To
bring in one more big Restoration gun to stress the diabolic connections of
Purcell's witches, compare their "Destruction's our delight" chorus with

> To do aught good never will be our task,
> But ever to do ill our sole delight

which is Satan in *Paradise Lost*, no less (I.159-60). Given all this, I see no
reason for making the witches in *Dido* anything other than menacingly sinister, though their energy and glee may well exhilarate and fascinate us. A way
to realize this in production is to take a leaf out of Franz Liszt's book. His way
of solving the problem of presenting the Spirit That Denies in the *Faust
Symphony* is to make the Mephistopheles scherzo a black parody of the opening Faust movement; and this can be applied usefully to production of the
witch scenes in *Dido*. After all, Tate and Purcell provide the structure: their
courtly scenes have a female protagonist singing mainly slow music, two girl
attendants with more animated music, a cheerful but hardly sensitive chorus
which sings simple dance numbers in the main, and one male soloist — a
voyager who loves and leaves. If you look at the witch scenes (including the
one with the sailors) you will find this structure repeated exactly, which can
hardly be accidental. Hence it posits an icy dignity for the Sorceress (no pantomime wicked fairy she) and means that in production the sentiments and
rituals of the court can be grotesquely guyed by the witches (widdershins
dances, sick-caricature mimes to accompany the Sorceress's prophecies and
provoke those ho-ho outbursts, etc.), a process to which Purcell's music gives
warrant in the Sailor's Song, where that lover-leaver's cynical libertinism at

> And silence their mourning
> With vows of returning
> But never intending to visit them more

is accompanied by a jaunty pre-echo of the familiar ground bass which will support Dido's aria of mourning at the climax of the opera. (By the way, I am not sure that Purcell and Tate meant their evil sisters to be the disadvantaged harridans, sluts and crones of downtown Carthage that some socially-minded producers choose nowadays to make them. Is there anything really demotic or *demi-mondaine* about their music? And you only have to compare the words they sing with those of Davenant's witches, or even those of Tate's own Mediterranean coven in *Brutus of Alba*, to realize that the sisters in *Dido*, however wayward, have definite class.)

8. ARE THERE FOUR SCENES IN *DIDO* OR FIVE?

The division into acts in *Dido and Aeneas* does not seem to me to be very helpful, and besides, the manuscripts and 1689 libretto differ over where the divisions come. It is better, I think, to conceive of the piece in four scenes — (I) "The Palace," (II) "The Cave," (III) "The Grove," and (IV) "The Ships" — each with its single inexorable line. Between scenes — always after some sort of triumphing dance and at least twice with the possibility of thunder and lightning from backstage — there should be a half-minute pause for the painted wings and shutters to change before the audience's eyes and for the audience to get a little of its breath back. Or are there five scenes? A footnote to the

Act the First. Scene: the Palace. Enter Dido and Belinda, and Train . . .
"A Room of Stait, with Statues & Bustoes," designed by Sir James Thornhill for Act I of Clayton's opera *Arsinoë*, Drury Lane 1705

Laurie/Dart performing edition says of the moment before Dido's final entry ("Your counsel all is urged in vain"), "the scene should change back to the Palace here, evidently." While granting that such a change could be made on the Restoration stage in a trice, I do not find it evident that it should happen at all, for two reasons. First, each new scene up to now has been preceded by an instrumental prelude and there is none (or at least none survives) at this point; second, there is a powerful theatrical irony if Dido and Aeneas quarrel grandly over parting on the same wharf on which the sailors and their witching molls have just been taking their "boozy short leave." Again, one can argue that it is quite wrong for the audience to be able to regain any breath here; and besides, running the action on allows the producer, if he is so minded, to keep his Sorceress on stage until the end of the Witches' Dance, then have her dismiss her sisters and for a split second share the stage with her anti-self the queen, who has come on to face her lover for the last time and then her death.

9. IS AENEAS A COMPLETE BOOBY?

If having Dido and the Sorceress twist eyebeams for an instant is allowable in an opera which has very little room for such production "points," so perhaps is encouraging the Sorceress and her two attendants to come gloating on stage (far *up* stage) half a minute early for their cue at "Then since our charms have sped" in the Grove scene, early enough to be visible to the audience while Aeneas, in soliloquy down front, is blaming the gods for his having to desert Dido. This emphasizes the extent to which Aeneas is a puppet in the witches' hands and, paradoxically perhaps, helps to maintain the audience's sympathy for him. Still, I would hesitate before telling an Aeneas that he is being literally upstaged during his climactic high F: the role has a pronounced enough reputation among baritones for unrewardingness as it is. Joseph Kerman speaks for the baritones in the often perceptive section on *Dido* in his *Opera as Drama* (1956), where he describes the Trojan prince as "a complete booby" (p. 56). But this is unjust, I think. True, Aeneas has no arias, not even a proper duet, and he does let the witches ride roughshod over him. But then it *is* Dido's opera and Aeneas is only significant as her loved seducer. There is no call for us to look at his head from within, as it were, as an aria would allow us to. Indeed, there is interesting evidence in the Eric Walter White essay I mentioned above that Purcell may have been offered the text for an Aeneas aria beginning

> Direct me, friends, what choice to make
> Since love and fame together press me

See, your royal guest appears:
How godlike is the form he bears!

Illustrations from the *Dissertatio de Actione Scenica* of Franciscus Lang, 1727

and either set it and then discarded the setting or declined to set it at all. As for letting the witches ride roughshod, it must be said in Aeneas's defense that he thinks that it is the gods he is letting subdue him, which is, after all, very pious. (There is nothing in the actual ultimatum of the false Mercury to suggest its falsity.) Then again, Aeneas is as handsome, brave and amorous as he is pious. So far, so positive. And he is the more interesting as a dramatic character because he is, in addition, so self-absorbed that he cannot see the complexities of others, certainly not of Dido. I suspect too that he is a rather selfish love-maker ("one night enjoyed . . ."), certainly too animal for the sensitive queen. How else is one supposed to take the monster's head on the bending spear (the only obligatory prop in the whole opera), which so troubles her that it beclouds her day?

10. IS THERE A CLEAR TIME-SCHEME IN THE OPERA?

The four lines "Go revel, ye Cupids, the day is your own," "Charge him sail tonight with all his fleet away," "Ere sunset shall most wretched prove," and "One night enjoyed, the next forsook" between them determine a time-scheme: the Palace scene takes place "once upon a time," the Cave scene in the early hours of the following morning, the Grove scene around the middle of the same day as the Cave scene, and the Ships scene that night. A few hours before curtain-up Aeneas has "sung" his "tale so strong and full of woe" to Dido and her court (another sore point with the baritones!). A vivid but simple lighting plot could present Scene I in an ever-increasing indoor daylight (*petite levée, grande levée*, diplomatic reception, cheerful festivity); Scene II as starting in the half-light of a chilly dawn and ending with something bright enough to drive the witches into their cave to avoid the glare of "this open air"; Scene III as an afternoon *fête champêtre* bathed in sunlight until the storm-clouds build up at the reference to the monster's head and then dominate and darken the grove till the end; and Scene IV as leading from a lurid post-storm sunset for the "boozy short leave" to moonlight ("Phoebe's pale deluding beams") at the unfurling of the sails. (Through the moonlight scurries the libretto's "Jack of the Lanthorn:" presumably the Sorceress's Puck/Ariel-like "trusty elf," who has exchanged the disguise of Mercury in which he has perplexed Aeneas for that of a will-o'-the-wisp to perplex Aeneas's shipmen. Ideas for staging this scene might well be provoked by looking at the Jack o'Lantern masque in Robert Stapylton's *Slighted Maid* of 1663, which Dennis Arundell describes in Chapter VI of *The Critic at the Opera*.)

11. HOW FAR SHOULD ELECTRICITY BE USED?

For sound effects, the electrical should and can be avoided. The thunder the manuscripts call for at the beginning and end of the Cave scene must be of the same order as the orchestral thunder in the middle of the Grove scene, which is to say Baroque-artificial — for preference made by cannon-balls in a thunder-run (see *The Oxford Companion to the Theatre* on this). For lighting effects the problem is greater. It is tempting to insist that the electrical should be avoided here too and (assuming an indoor performance) the whole thing lit with candles. But unless the venue is one where public fire regulations do not apply, one cannot avoid electricity. So the person on the board needs to be constrained to work within the limits of simulating what a well-equipped private Restoration theatre that inherited the masquing traditions of the Stuart court could do, which means in effect simple pre-sets, perhaps some atmospheric coloring and a limited amount of general fading; but next-to-no isolated spots and no aspiring to Broadway-musical virtuosity.

12. WHAT DOES ONE DO WITH THE CHORUS?

I am tempted to ignore my own advice about lighting during Dido's two great
arias over ground bass, which seem to be directed at Belinda and perhaps at
the Second Woman but hardly at the court *en masse*. Surely there is a case
here for bringing the follow-spot up on the heroine and fading the courtiers
down very low. Maybe; but it is not an impressive case, just a weak *ad hoc*
solution to one part of the general problem of *Dido's* almost omnipresent
chorus. It is a problem which has been variously tackled. You can read in the
columns of *Opera*— these examples are from Vols. XVII and XXIV — of the
chess-game that once went on at Cambridge during Dido's "Peace and I are
strangers grown," and of the Kabuki stylization for a stationary chorus at
Tokyo, and of the producer at Dallas who chose to banish the chorus to the

pit. I would suggest that a more moderate course is more satisfying and apropos. Take the case of Dido's Lament. The music earlier in this scene has unfortunately not given any signal for the entry of the courtiers, yet they need to be on stage in time for their "Great minds against themselves conspire" and hence they are present when the queen dies. Their arrival, I think, needs to be tactful, unobtrusive and piecemeal: some with Belinda and the Second Woman at Dido's own entry; others with Aeneas when he makes his crestfallen appearance (which must surely mirror his more cocksure arrival in Scene I); the rest—individually cued and always with somewhere to go—between that entry and "Great minds" itself. Such comings and goings of Dido's court can be easily achieved if the most authoritative of the chorus men is given the role of Dido's chamberlain or major domo, her equivalent of the Sorceress's "trusty elf"; so all that needs to happen at "Thy hand, Belinda" is for the chamberlain to avert his head and the rest of the court will follow suit: there is no need for general fades. (It helps too, if two other chorus men are cast as confidant-lieutenants to Aeneas. On a level of symmetry this gives the prince a similar retinue to those of Dido and the Sorceress, and it also allows a boyfriend apiece to Belinda and Second Woman in the Grove scene.) Just as it is the conductor's problem to balance the necessity for each scene in *Dido* to be as ongoing as a symphonic movement with the other necessity that every dramatic moment be put across with maximum intensity, so it is the producer's problem to achieve a clear, unfussy line for each scene while at the same time ensuring that the figures on stage are never just standing about (something the music never does). Court protocol, together with a carefully worked out demeanor for the heroine and the principle that the activity of the witches is a deadly mockery of both, will provide a reliable source for all needful business.

13. MONSTERS AND FOUNTAINS: HOW MUCH DOES ONE STRESS THE SYMBOLS?

My facetious mention of Osbert Lancaster's *Waste Land* parody earlier has its serious point. After all, the *Vénus tout entière à sa proie attachée* of Racine's *Phèdre* could almost be the motto of Purcell's opera. In a rather different sense from Charpentier's *Actéon*, *Dido* too is an "opéra de chasse": the symbolism of erotic pursuit and capture is central to it. "Pursue thy conquest, Love!" says Belinda in Scene I, and "Fate forbids what you pursue" is Dido's first word when Aeneas comes courting. The loving pursuit finds its emblem in a courtly hunting party ("The queen and he are now in chase . . . So fair the game, so rich the sport"), during which one of Dido's women sings of a virgin goddess's lover fatally "pursued by his own hounds" and Aeneas compares the boar he has caught to the one which gored to death the boy the goddess of

Thanks to these lovesome vales,
These desert hills and dales.

Proscenium and three pairs of landscape wings designed by John Webb for Davenant's
Siege of Rhodes, 1656

love doted on. These are bad omens which, with the sexual roles reversed, are
soon fulfilled: it is Dido who is the Actaeon/Adonis trapped and destroyed
("One night enjoyed, the next forsook"). And as soon as the quondam virgin
queen, resting during the chase near Diana's fountain after a night of love
with Aeneas, sees the bleeding monster's head on the prince's spear, she
"discovers too, too late" what has happened to her. At that moment someone
walks over her grave:

> The skies are clouded. Hark, how thunder
> Rends the mountain oaks asunder!

I would not suggest that the symbolism of *Vénus et sa proie* is very clearly
worked out in Tate's libretto. But I do think that it would be as unwise to pooh-
pooh it altogether as to turn the Grove scene into an expressionist jamboree
on the strength of it. The producer must be tactful. Until the weather breaks,
the gathering at the grove is a civilized rite-cum-entertainment, as the Sorceress—called there Ragusa—makes clear in Act III of Tate's *Brutus of Alba*.

> When the sports are done
> The Court repairs to the *Diana* Fountain,
> To worship there the Goddess of the Woods

And drink of the cool Stream . . .
When they have drunk, an entertainment follows . . .
Heark, the Stagg's faln, and now the Court comes on
To th'Fountain to perform the *Sylvan* Rites;
'Tis time we were preparing for the Storm.

The *Dido* gathering should be suave and elegant but not prettified or frivolous. Actaeon's pain is still in the air, and the climax of the Second Woman's marvellous aria makes us feel it. (In another sense John Blow's *Venus and Adonis*, only about six years old when *Dido* was given, is still in the air too: Aeneas's recitative about the boar is surely on one level an allusion to it.) Beyond this, two things are worth noting where staging is concerned. First, the couplet beginning "the skies are clouded" is the only thing Dido sings in the whole scene; so it must be carefully prepared for if it is not to seem a very English conversation-filler. Second, the couplet is soon followed by her leaving the grove without Aeneas, which probably means that she has avoided him since the couplet and that any attempts he may have made to come to her side have been thwarted by the jostling of the town-bound crowd (rather as in the final reel of *Les Enfants du Paradis*). Hence a lot of dramatic emphasis is thrown onto that boar's head on the bending spear, which must be Baroque-heraldic, sinister, mildly phallic and quite unfunny. Rule I for *Dido*-producers is "Find a good maker of boars' heads." If you can't, do *The Seagull* instead. . . .

14. WHO DANCES WHAT?

The music of *Dido* is very gestural. (If you feel no muscular response to the four orchestral bars in the middle of the chorus "To the hills and the vales" or to the viola line under the Sorceress's phrase "whom we *hate*" in the Cave scene or to the queen's "No repentance shall reclaim" in her quarrel with Aeneas, think even more seriously about switching to Chekhov.) Hence the opera will support expansive and eloquent movement, from which various formal measures such as the Triumphing Dance and antic pantomimes such as the Jack o'Lantern episode can take off. The libretto and manuscripts do not make it clear who did the dancing in the original performances. I see no reason why the queen and prince should not dance a private "Gittars Chacony" and "Gitter Ground a Dance" in the Palace and Grove scenes (if those numbers are going to be included), and it is effective if they join publicly in the court's Triumphing Dance after the two rogue bars in the middle of the number when the first violins start to play the ground bass. For the rest, Mr. Priest probably taught the many dances called for to some of his young gentlewomen and their gentlemen friends, but whether those gentlefolk were, or should be, the same girls and boys who sing the choruses is not clear. Perhaps the likeli-

A Dance to entertain Aeneas by Dido's women . . .
Late 17th-century costume design in the manner of Jean Bérain

hood is a separate dance troupe: this is suggested by the request of the full coven that "Nymphs of Carthage" should lead the pleasing, easing dance at the end of the Grove scene and by the libretto's stage direction that the Cupids who appear in the clouds after the chorus "Great minds against themselves conspire" should dance either during or after the chorus "With drooping wings you Cupids come." What *is* clear is that the dancing should be Baroque-based—Priest, not Petipa. Young Pavlovas need not apply, though applicants will need to be pretty versatile to cope with the "masquing" and "antimasquing" dance styles called for.

15. IS DIDO A VIRGIN QUEEN AT THE START AND
WHEN DOES INTIMACY TAKE PLACE?

Forgive the forensic questions in what, after all, is a very discreet opera, but the producer and principals presumably do need to know the answers. If I read the libretto aright, with its wholesale modifications of Vergil, the opera gives us a study of a virgin queen married to her nation and suppressing the urge to personal fulfilment through love because of an awareness that it might be divisive of her country or of her attention to her country. In spite of this she chooses, blamelessly but self-laceratingly, to accept a dashing young nobleman as her lover. (The closeness of so much of this to the Britten/Plomer *Gloriana* is intriguing, and I doubt it is wholly coincidental, since Britten started to compose *Gloriana* the year after he had made his edition of *Dido* and conducted several performances of it. In some of these, the tragic lovers were played by Joan Cross and Peter Pears, who went on to create the roles of Elizabeth and Essex in *Gloriana*. The fact that the former addresses her sage counsellor Robert Cecil at one point as her "trusty elf" is the least of the parallels between the two operas.) It is perhaps a flaw in Purcell's opera — it certainly makes it difficult for the performers — that the precise moment of Dido's acceptance of Aeneas's love near the end of the first scene is not made musically clear, though one must admit that it is hard to imagine any words on the subject by the queen, and a love duet (something remotely related to the finale of *L'Incoronazione di Poppea*) would give too much parity of interest to Aeneas. The moment of acceptance has to come somewhere between Belinda's observation that the queen's "eyes/Confess the flame her tongue denies" and the chorus's "Let the triumphs of love and of beauty be shown" about thirty seconds later, which does not give much time for the necessary piece of simple but eloquent mime. There is more time, of course, if one inserts "A Dance Gittars Chacony" at this point — something the 1689 libretto asks for but Purcell's surviving score does not provide. Could it be that at the first performance Aeneas led Dido in a formal courtship-and-acceptance dance here, accompanied by a much scaled down band to suggest the intimacy of the moment and, since so accompanied, not needing the composer to write the part out beforehand? Support for this would come from the fact that the only other unsurviving guitar dance, the "ground" in the Grove scene, also comes at a point where the now united royal lovers could aptly execute a stately but private *pas de deux*, i.e., just before the Second Woman's Actaeon aria. Certainly without these guitar movements the hero and heroine are allowed puritanically little *tendresse* on stage. The *tendresse* off-stage follows Scene I. When the lovers leave after "Go revel, ye Cupids," it is to set out for some notional hunting lodge where they spend the night, their love-making coinciding with the announcement by the Sorceress that she has devised "a mischief that shall make all Carthage flame." (It is, by the way, an interesting example of the opera's wry use of Vergil that the first scene's Triumphing Dance should immediately be followed by thunder and lightning and a scene-change to a secluded cave. Every Restoration schoolboy would know that Dido and Aeneas were about to enter and take shelter together. Instead we are presented with the Sorceress, Dido's destructive anti-self.)

16. HOW DOES DIDO DIE?

Dido's death for Metastasio and Sarro in *Didone Abbandonata* (1724) is al-most as histrionic and spectacular as Brünnhilde's for Wagner in *Götterdäm-merung*: she throws herself frantically into the burning ruins of her palace just before it is overwhelmed by a raging sea. But Dido's dying for Tate and Purcell is almost as ambiguous as Isolde's in *Tristan*. With Isolde it is not so much death as transfiguration. With Dido the chorus's references to her tomb and drooping-winged Cupids assure us that death has come, but when and how is not definite. "When" is something a sensitive producer will have vir-tually to choreograph to relate to the two final statements of the ground bass of her Lament. "How" is more problematical. She is clearly resolved to die and her heart is near breaking-point. But earlier in the scene she seems to have threatened suicide ("To death I'll fly if longer you delay") and earlier still the Sorceress has prophesied that she will "bleed." The only consistent and tactful solution, I think, is that she should produce or find a small dagger and pierce her breast with it firmly but unmelodramatically during the or-chestral conclusion to the Lament, acting the scene as if the tiniest physical wound would be sufficient to dispatch someone whose vitality has been almost drained away by emotional suffering. The music will do the rest. As for the dagger, it is worth noting that it breaks the rule that there are no essential props in *Dido*, with the grand exception of the monster's head on the bending spear. I have found it effective in production—and a way to maintain that austerity, as well as to provide Dido with a kind of tomb to die on and perhaps have roses scattered over—if, during the antic Jack o'Lantern dance earlier in the Ships scene, some of Aeneas's sailors bring in the hero's spear, helmet, breastplate and sea-chests *en route* for his ship, but are scared away by the witches before they can take them off again. This means that the queen can take a dagger from the breastplate, then sink onto the chests (less far to fall than the floor in very slow, quiet music) and die beneath a hollow Aeneas-image. It happens that such a piece of business is also fairly faithful to Vergil's account of Dido's death, for what that is worth.

*   *   *

Purcell's opera is capable of being presented on the stage in very many different ways. It can be given with the singers seated on chairs and making but few movements; or it can be mounted as they mount the operas of Gluck in Paris. And then there is another way of mounting it; that is in the more modern and up-to-date manner. And then there is the way of the individualist. This is Mr. Craig's way. It is always different, and when he produces a play or an opera he follows no old-fashioned manner, and no up-to-date manner; he does it in a manner which is personal and which is not to be imitated and which cannot be imitated.

This is "Allen Carric" (alias Gordon Craig) in *The Mask* for January 1909 praising Craig's production of *Dido* nine years after the event. And though my way with the opera is clearly very different from his—when W. B. Yeats celebrates "Gordon Craig's purple backcloth that made Dido and Aeneas seem wandering on the edge of eternity," I want to replace the lovers with Pelléas and Mélisande—the terms of his discussion seem to me sound. I certainly agree that the producer must do things "in a manner which is personal," but I doubt whether the personalness need or should be as private, intransigent, perhaps irresponsible, as Craig implies. My personal manner, as I hope these sixteen investigations have shown, springs from an attempt to marry two beliefs: first, that if an "early" opera is any good, it is because it is a memorable embodiment in sound and gesture of something important for us as an audience now; second, that the intent of a seventeenth- or eighteenth-century opera composer in providing his blueprint of notes was inextricably and happily bound up with the resources and conventions of the librettists, choreographers, scenographers and stage-managers he worked with, and can only fully come alive when they do. I recommend these beliefs with an assurance that their marriage, if achieved by sixty-nine different producers working with different companies in different theatres, would not lead to productions which were carbon copies of each other or of that unrepeatable first night at Chelsea, Versailles, Mantua or wherever. What it would do would be to give every single one of those nine-and-sixty productions a better chance of being *right* than many an early opera we see around nowadays.

Curtis Price is a Reader in Historical Musicology at the Faculty of Music, King's College, London. He earned his Ph.D. at Harvard University and has been a Frank Knox Travelling Fellow and a Woodrow Wilson scholar. The recipient of Guggenheim, NEH and ACLS grants, Dr. Price has received the Albert Einstein Award and the Edward J. Dent Medal awarded by the Royal Musical Association "for an outstanding contribution to musicology." He is the author of *Music in the Restoration Theatre* (1979) and *Henry Purcell and the London Stage* (1984).